# FOLLOW ME

*The Fourteen Most Important
Days of Jesus' Ministry in a
Unified Narrative*

## BY
# WALTER ZIGLAR

Cover illustration in watercolor by
## HERMAN RAYMOND

MERIWETHER PUBLISHING LTD.
Colorado Springs, Colorado

4/96

**Meriwether Publishing Ltd., Publisher**
**P.O. Box 7710**
**Colorado Springs, CO 80933**

$8.95

**Editor: Arthur Zapel**
**Assistant editor: Pat Middleton**
**Typesetting: Sharon Garlock**
**Cover illustration: Herman Raymond**
**Book design: Michelle Gallardo**

© Copyright MCMLXXXVIII Meriwether Publishing Ltd.
Printed in the United States of America
First Edition

Quotations adapted with permission of Macmillan Publishing Company from *New Testament in Modern English* (Revised Edition) by J. B. Phillips. Copyright © 1958, 1960, 1972 by J. B. Phillips.

**Library of Congress Cataloging-in-Publication Data**

Ziglar, Walter.
    Follow me.

    Bibliography: p.
    1. Jesus Christ—Biography—Sources, Biblical.
I. Title.
BT299.2.Z54    1988              232.9'5              88-13527
ISBN 0-916260-56-9

Bookstore

*To Sharon, Katie and Matthew*

# The Fourteen Most Important "Days"

*To simplify and highlight the key moments of Jesus' holy mission, the author has chosen the term "Day" to group a series of significant events. This time designation, "Day," does not represent any twenty-four hour span but only a topical period as one division of Jesus' total three-and-one-half year ministry.*

# Table of Contents

# Foreword

In the writing and structuring of this book, the author consulted several translations of the Holy Bible for a clear perspective of Jesus Christ's ministry as told in the New Testament. Especially helpful in the development of the dialog were the most accepted Scripture sources: *The Holy Bible,* Authorized King James Version, first published in 1611, revised AD 1881-1885 and AD 1901, and *The Holy Bible, American Standard Version,* edited by the American Revision Committee, 1901.

For easy reading in the context of a narrative style, the author paraphrased some of the biblical verses but with careful attention not to change their scriptural integrity.

The use of the personal pronoun "he" in reference to our Lord and Savior, Jesus Christ, has not been capitalized in the narrative text of this book. This is in accordance with current usage of most Christian periodical and book publishers, and the publisher's bible: *A Manual of Style,* Twelfth Edition, Revised by the University of Chicago Press. This usage implies no disrespect or irreverance of our Lord, Jesus Christ, but is employed for purposes of easier reading. The author does not share the publisher's preference in this usage.

*The Publisher*

# Map Illustrations

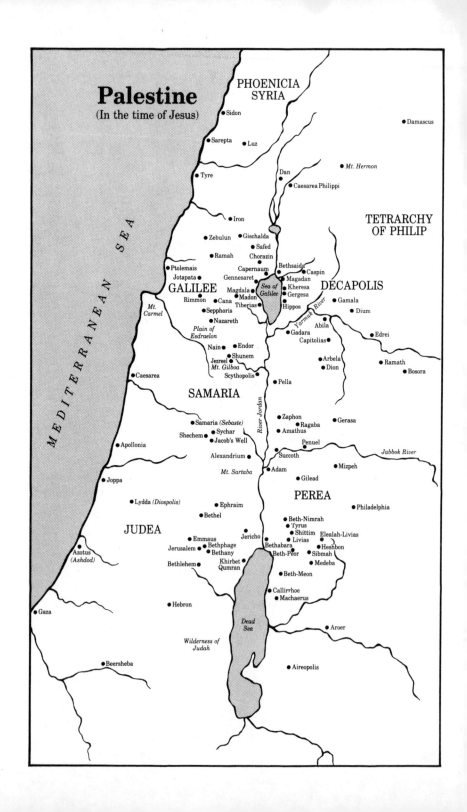

# Palestine
## (In the time of Jesus)

PHOENICIA
SYRIA

MEDITERRANEAN SEA

• Sidon
• Damascus

• Sarepta    • Luz

• Mt. Hermon

• Tyre
Dan •
• Caesarea Philippi

• Iron

TETRARCHY
OF PHILIP

• Zebulun   • Gischalda
• Safed
• Ramah   Chorazin
Capernaum   • Bethsaida
• Ptolemais
Jotapata •   Gennesaret   • Caspin
GALILEE   Magadan •
Sea of    • Kheresa
Magdala   Galilee   • Gergesa
Rimmon   • Madon   Hippos •
• Cana   Tiberias •
• Sepphoris
• Nazareth

DECAPOLIS
• Gamala
• Dium

Yarmuk River

Mt.
Carmel

Plain of
Esdraelon
Nain •   • Endor
Jezreel •   • Shunem
Mt. Gilboa
Scythopolis •

Abila
• Gadara
Capitolias •

• Edrei

• Arbela
• Dion
• Ramath
• Bosora

• Caesarea

SAMARIA

River Jordan

• Pella

• Samaria (Sebaste)
• Sychar
Shechem •   • Jacob's Well

• Zaphon
• Ragaba
Amathus

• Gerasa

Jabbok River

• Apollonia

Alexandrium •

Penuel

• Joppa

Mt. Sartaba
• Adam

Succoth

• Mizpeh

• Gilead

PEREA

• Lydda (Diospolis)
• Ephraim
• Bethel

JUDEA

Azotus
(Ashdod) •

• Emmaus
Jerusalem •   • Bethphage
• Bethany
Bethlehem •   Khirbet
Qumran

Jericho
•

• Beth-Nimrah
• 'Tyrus
• Shittim   Elealah-Livias
• Livias
Bethabara
Beth-Peor •

• Philadelphia

• Heshbon
• Sibmah
• Medeba

• Beth-Meon

• Gaza

• Hebron

Dead
Sea

• Callirrhoe
• Machaerus

• Aroer

Wilderness of
Judah

• Beersheba

• Aireopolis

# Prologue

*"Follow me,"* said Jesus, *"and I will make you the fishers of men."* (Matthew 4:19) And his apostles did just that.

Two of them, Matthew and John, actually wrote about their experiences with the Master. If these were the only narratives recorded in the New Testament, our knowledge of Jesus' travels and ministry would be sketchy at best.

Thanks, however, to collaborative narratives by the council, Mark, who accompanied the apostles as a youth and Luke, the physician, who interviewed scores of eyewitnesses to Jesus' ministry, we have a far more comprehensive account of his three-and-one-half years of public life. These accounts of Mark and Luke, coupled with Matthew's narrative, comprise the Synoptic Gospels which can be cross-referenced by New Testament readers.

The apostle, John, having written from his own memory at the age of 99, brought to light a number of episodes in the life of Jesus that were omitted by previous authors.

"Follow Me" is an attempt to corrolate these accounts of the Master's life into a single, unified narrative spanning a period over three years (January AD 27 - April AD 30) of public ministry.

The difficulty in formulating a single narrative on the 14 most important days in the life of Jesus results from a number of omissions by the gospel authors themselves. For instance, although not included in this narrative, the synoptic gospels record Peter's denial of Christ in the courtyard of Caiaphas, omitting his appearance in front of Annas, but the apostle who witnessed these events, John, recorded Peter's denial in the courtyard of Annas. John's account is accurate if we can assume no animals were allowed within the city gates of Jerusalem under Roman law, and since Caiaphas' palace was within the city gates, no cock could have crowed. We also know that in such delicate matters as a trial on blasphemy the Romans always dealt with Annas first, and since his palace was not far from the garden of Gethsemane, we must assume Jesus went there first as recorded by the apostle, John Zebedee.

There were several other significant events which were recorded by only one of the apostles. This in no way diminishes the credibility of these accounts, as Jesus told various apostles on a number of occasions to "tell no man."

Luke, the physician, records several accounts which we may assume were purposely excluded by the apostles and young John Mark\*; one of these accounts was the healing of the widow's son at Nain. Another such healing not recorded in Matthew, Mark and John, presumably because Jesus told his apostles not to tell anyone, was the healing of the ten lepers at Amathus on the borders of Samaria. Another incident not recorded by the apostles but found in Luke was that of Jesus curing a man suffering from dropsy. This incident occurred on the Sabbath, in the home of a leading Pharisee in Philadelphia. The following parable on the "Great Supper" was also omitted by the authors Matthew, Mark and John, as was the story of "The Good Samaritan."

There were a number of times when not all of the apostles were in attendance to witness the teachings and healings of the Master. One such time was during the "Feast of Tabernacles" when John Mark was absent. Matthew was also absent during this event, having gone over to a village on the eastern slopes of Mount Gilboa to secure lodging for the apostles. Although these authors were not present to personally witness the Master's teaching in the temple, many thousands of people did as recorded by the apostle, John (Chapters 7 and 8). John also recorded the sermon on the "Good Shepherd," (John 10:1-16) but it was omitted by the other authors.

John devoted all of chapter nine to the encounter of Jesus healing the blind man near the pool of Siloam, but this entire incident was never recorded in the Synoptic Gospels.

Some of the most significant events in the apostles' association with Jesus seem to have been excluded by the youngest of all the apostles, John Zebedee. For instance, John makes no mention of Jesus' baptism and the forty days of communion with the Father. There is no mention of the "Mount of Transfiguration" episode, which John himself witnessed along with his brother, James, and Peter, and yet, this event is heavily documented in the Synoptic Gospels.

---

*\*John Mark, although too young to be an apostle, was the constant companion to the apostles from their first preaching at the Jordan ford near Jericho (except for the trip to Phoenicia) right up until the Master's betrayal.*

On the other hand, one of the most extraordinary events in all the apostles' association with Jesus was the resurrection of Lazarus from the dead. This momentous event was well documented by John (Chapter 11) but excluded from the synoptic gospels — Matthew, Mark and Luke.

As already mentioned, some of the omissions in the Bible narratives were the result of Jesus' specific command to his apostles but not to his followers, those eyewitness observers who subsequently reported to Luke.

On at least one occasion, additional material was thought to be added to these narratives. Very early in the second century a Jewish apocalyptic about the Messiah written by one Selta, who was attached to the court of the Emperor Caligula, was bodily copied into the Matthew gospel. These writings of Selta had to do with the account of the 10 virgins and the kingdom of heaven. One last matter concerning the chronology of this narrative has to do with the birth date of Jesus. Although the events, the seasons and the months are in chronological order right up until Jesus' last temple discourse two days before his crucifixion, the following information may be of some clarification in pinpointing the year and the month of his birth.

Although scholars over the years have debated the actual date of Jesus' birth, there is sufficient evidence pointing to the late summer of the year 7 BC.

On one point, all scholars agree, that Jesus was an infant when Herod decreed that all boy babies under the age of two should be put to death. The slaughter of these infants took place in October of the year 6 BC. Herod had the decency to die two years later in the year 4 BC. These events would then place Jesus' birth in the year 6 BC or before.

Now Luke tells us (Luke 2:1-6) that Jesus was born during the reign of Caesar Augustus, when Quirinius was governor of Syria. But Quirinius was legate of Syria between 6 and 12 AD. The confusion lies in the fact that Augustus had decreed that a census be taken of the Roman empire, and Luke, the author of the gospel Luke (AD 82), interpreted this as the one taken when Quirinius was governor of Syria. According to the first century historian, Josephus (Wars II, 8), there was a census by Quirinius in Judea in the year 6-7 AD.

The matter of the census is cleared up by the Christian historian, Tertullian, who records a census by Saturninus, governor of Syria 8-7 BC. This was, in fact, the same census the "good doctor" (Luke) ascribed to Quirinius (Adv. Marcionem IV 19).

Actually, Caesar Augustus had decreed that the census take place in the year 8 BC, but as a favor to Herod, he allowed the Jews of Palestine to register a year later in 7 BC. Accordingly, Joseph and Mary set out in the late summer months of this year to register for this census in Jerusalem.

It was in this same year, 7 BC, that there occurred an extraordinary conjunction of the planets Jupiter and Saturn in the month of May. Similar conjunctions occurred later in this year which may well account for the bright star (star of Bethlehem) witnessed by so many.

This may be all well and good, scholars say, but how then does one account for the fact that Luke records (Luke 3:1) that Jesus was baptized in the fifteenth year of the reign of Tiberius, presumably the year AD 29 since Augustus died in the year 14 AD?

It should be recalled that Tiberius ruled as co-emperor with Augustus (Suetonius, "Tiberius" 121) for two-and-a-half years, having coins struck in his honor in October of the year, AD 11. So the year of his baptism was actually the year AD 26, when he was thirty-one-and-a-half, the same year Pontius Pilate began his rule as governor of Judea. This documented evidence effectively substantiates Jesus' birthdate as that of 7 BC.

It is generally recognized that Joseph journeyed south in the late summer, probably in August. The December 25th birthdate was a later compromise which came about in the first century when the apostle, Paul, sought to convert the Mithraic followers into Christianity. Mithra, the sun deity, was born of a virgin on December 25th, and this holy day (natalis invicti solis), although miscalculated, was thought to be the beginning of the winter solstice.

To win these converts to Christianity, Paul chose this festive date to coincide with the birth of Jesus. Ironically, until the fourth century, the eastern church celebrated Jesus' birthdate on January 6, charging their western brethren with sun worship and idolatry.

It makes little difference when our Lord was born, but the dates I have selected for this narrative, to my knowledge, most accurately reflect those months and days in which Jesus actually preached and taught.

In formulating this narrative on fourteen of the most important events in the ministry of Jesus, this author attempted to choose those days and events which had some spiritual significance or universal truth that Jesus imparted to his apostles and disciples for their future dissemination.

The primary purpose of this narrative is to capture those most intimate moments shared by the Master and his apostles. These were the conversations on the road, in the homes and gardens of his friends, and around campfires in the evening.

Admittedly, some of the major events in the life of Jesus are excluded, such as his baptism on the Jordan, the turning of water into wine, etc. Of these events we are all aware, but it is the moments leading up to these events, the moments of apprehension as well as exhilaration between Jesus, his apostles, his followers, and even his enemies, I have attempted to capture in this book.

What were the simple truths he taught in intimate discussion — those revelations of the Father's character gathered through personal contact?

Moses, in his day, gave to his people what God directed him to give — the Ten Commandments. For the next 1,200 years, written postulates and laws of the elders governed the Jewish people, until living truth was presented to the planet in the person of Jesus of Nazareth — the Son of God and Son of Man.

The religion of Jesus was wholly based on the living of his bestowal life on earth. When Jesus departed from this world, he left behind no books, laws, or other forms of human organization affecting the religious life of the individual. He repeatedly warned his apostles against the formulation of creeds and the establishment of traditions as a means of guiding and controlling believers in the gospel of the Kingdom.

Until Jesus, God had only revealed himself through Moses as the infinite "I am," and when pressed for further revelation of himself, it was only disclosed that "I am that I am."

But through his personal ministry and teachings, Jesus, the Son of God, could truly say:

*I am the bread of life.* (John 6:35, 48)
*I am the living water.* (John 4:14, 7:37-38)
*I am the light of the world.* (John 8:12, 9:5)
*I am the open door to eternal salvation.* (John 10:9)

*I am the good shepherd.* (John 10:11, 14)
*I am the resurrection and the life.* (John 11:25)
*I am the way, the truth and the life.* (John 14:6)
*I am the true vine; you are the branches.* (John 15:1, 5)

These are the representations Jesus made to his apostles and his followers which were an enlargement of the living revelation of God to all generations.

It is these revelations of the Master's infinite and loving character as told in conversation and in sermon to his intimate associates, his followers and his enemies that truly bridge the gap between the finite and the infinite — man and God.

These truths lie at the heart of the Master's teachings and are the substance of this narrative on his life and teachings.

## Introduction

In the year 7BC, unceremoniously, a child was born; an event that was relatively insignificant to the community of Nazareth, except to the parents of one Joshua ben Joseph.

Although born of average parents, Joshua was not an average child; he was a child of destiny. He would live approximately thirty-five years on this planet, teaching and preaching and ministering to the people of his day.

In less than four years of public ministry, Joshua, whose Greek name was Jesus, would forever change in the minds of men their spiritual relationship to God, their heavenly Father.

Over the past 2,000 years, there has been more written and said about this Jesus of Nazareth than any other personality ever to walk the planet. And yet scholars estimate that the entire Bible only covers about fifty days of the life of Jesus. The first thirty years of his existence are hardly mentioned at all, yet the

1

ideals of his life and teachings have dominated the art and literature and ethics of western civilization for twenty centuries.

His disciples called him Master and we have come to know him as the Son of God incarnate as the Son of Man, Christ — the anointed one. More so, millions of Christians throughout the world have come to know him, not only in a literal sense, but on a personal basis, as a reality in human experience.

To those who knew him in the flesh, his character was flawless and unassailable as one might conceptualize God on earth to be.

But why did this deity choose to incarnate as a mortal on such an apparently insignificant planet in God's universe? What was his mission and what was his message? Did he come to build an empire on earth or to establish a kingdom of God upon the hearts of men? Did he come to give man written postulates, much as Moses did, or did he come to teach truth by living example? Did he come to establish a church with doctrines and creeds — to enslave men with ritual, or did he come to show men by his life and teachings, a living faith — to liberate them with the joy of living?

Did he come to legislate or to enlighten? Did he come to frighten them with the fear of God or to lure them with the love of God? Was his message one of repentance from sin and eternal damnation as was John before him, or was it one of love — to love one another as he loves us and that salvation is a gift of the Father available to all who choose to do his will?

Did his teachings dwell on the negative of sin and guilt or stress the positive of love and service?

Did he reveal to us a God of wrath and retribution and did he preach God's condemnation, or did he proclaim God's forgiveness — God's eternal mercy?

One thing is for certain, the Son of God brought to this planet the highest revelation man could possibly conceive of the heavenly Father. And this revelation was the product of his public ministry in preaching the gospel — the fatherhood of God and the brotherhood of man. As he loves us, we are to love one another. This was his message.

Before Jesus came to this world, man's concept of God was to view him anthropomorphically on the order of human personality traits, i.e., a stern, harsh, jealous, vengeful God of wrath, willing to punish his people at the slightest provocation.

In the Old Testament days of Samuel, the children of Abraham really believed that Yahweh created both good and evil. This is best illustrated in the passage of Samuel (2 Sam. 24:1) which states, *And the anger of the Lord was kindled against Israel, so much so that he moved David against them saying go number Israel and Judah.*

As the concept of the nature of God evolved towards a more compassionate God, later Jewish authors eliminated evil from God's creative prerogatives, as evidenced in 1 Chronicles, (1 Chron. 21:1). Here we see in a narrative of the same event that, *Satan stood up against Israel and provoked David to number Israel.* In short, God had created choice, to do his will or to transgress his will.

From one generation to the next man's concept of God would grow, eventually culminating in Jesus' revelation of a God of unbounding love and mercy.

In the days of Moses, however, the wrath of God prevailed. God was to be feared as he damned his enemies. The God of Moses' day sent evil spirits to dominate the souls of his enemies (Judges 9:23). He prospered his own and obedient children, while he cursed and visited dire judgments upon all others.

Eventually this wrath of God grew into divine wisdom, but seldom during these times was a God of love and mercy known to the Jewish people.

Although the prophets revealed a higher concept of Yahweh, this progressive evolution of the more divine manifestations of God's personality was slow to embed itself in the minds of the Jewish religious leaders.

It was Amos who first attacked the egotistic doctrine of the "chosen people," proclaiming as he did the "God of all nations" and warning the Israelites that ritual must not take the place of righteousness. For this wisdom he was stoned to death.

Oh, how history must repeat itself. Some 2,000 years later Girolamo Savonarola would publicly condemn the church at Rome for its evil abuses. For his vocal criticism, he was hung and burned at the stake.

Hosea followed Amos and his universal God of justice by preaching forgiveness through repentance, not by sacrifice.

Isaiah taught the eternal nature of God, his infinite wisdom, his unchanging perfection of reliability.

By the time of Micah and Obadiah the priesthood had well

entrenched itself in Jewish society, and although these two fearless prophets boldly denounced the priest-ridden ritual of the Hebrews and fearlessly attacked the whole sacrificial system, it was to no avail.

It was Micah who said, *Shall I come before God with burnt offerings? Will the Lord be pleased with a thousand rams or with ten thousand rivers of oil? Shall I give my first born for my transgressions, the fruit of my body for the sin of my soul? He has shown thee, O man, what is good; and what does the Lord require of you but to do justly and to love mercy and to walk humbly with your God.* (Micah 6:6-8)

Had it not been for the stubborn resistance of the priests, these two wise teachers would have overthrown the whole bloody ceremonial of the Hebrew ritual of worship, some 500 years before the coming of Christ.

And so it was, right on down to the times of Jesus, that the Jewish people were tenaciously held in ritual bondage by a tradition bound priesthood.

It was to these people Jesus would come to teach and to enlighten in the truths of the heavenly kingdom — the Kingdom of God.

Jesus would reveal to man a Creator God of every good and perfect purpose, wholly devoid of fear and enmity. Without wrath, man no longer had to live in the fear of God, only in the love of God.

But who was this gentle Galilean and how was he able to spiritually transform the men of his day, even to the point of risking crucifixion for his sake?

His life and his ministry were of matchless wonderment. But what was this ministry really like? How did it affect the people of his day? What kind of lasting impression did it leave upon them? Were they truly transformed individuals willing to give up their lives even after he had left them in the flesh?

I have often wondered how great it would have been to live with Jesus, or would it? How many of us would be willing to die for our faith today? If confronted with torture and crucifixion, would we accept the fate of Amos and Savonarola? If being a Christian meant facing lions in the arena, might we not hedge a bit on our commitment to Christ? Possibly, but not in Jesus' day, for it was well-nigh impossible to be neutral to him. To the vast majority of the people he came in contact with, he would forever change their lives, transforming them from complacent mediocrity to that of dynamic service in the Jesus brotherhood. To a handful of others, his avowed enemies, whose hearts were turned to stone, he was an object of hate and scorn and most importantly a threat to their existence. They would plot his death with the obsession and intensity, and single-mindedness of purpose as the Third Reich.

His crucifixion and subsequent resurrection are well documented and provide living proof as to his message of salvation for all who believe in him. But what about his life and teachings? Were they not the example of living truth he brought to the people of his day, truth that is as fresh today as it was 2,000 years ago? If we could return to those times what could we learn from our Lord that would change our lives as it did the lives of his followers? Was his mere presence transformative, or was it his message, or both? One thing is for certain, once having met him, peoples' lives were never the same. Whether it was Nalda, the woman at the well; the harlot who washed his feet with her hair; Zaccheus, the publican; Legion, the lunatic; Jairus, the leader of the Capernaum synagogue; Nicodemus, an elder of the Sanhedrin; Rebecca of Sepphoris; Mary Magdalene; Amatha; Peter's mother-in-law; Cornelius, the Roman soldier; John Mark, the chore boy; or even Pontius Pilate who said, "I find no fault in this man," all whose lives he touched were transformed by his majestic personality.

The key to Jesus' successful ministry was his total sincerity and his genuine interest in his fellow man. He was never in a hurry and always took time to comfort hungry minds and minister to thirsty souls as he passed by. He dispensed health and scattered happiness naturally and gracefully as he journeyed through life. He literally went about doing good.

If it were possible just once to step back into history, many a Christian would choose the opportunity to visit with Jesus, to live life as he lived it, to experience his teachings first-hand, to just be in his physical presence. How exhilarating it must have been to have known him in person as the Son of Man; God incarnate. Since this is a manifest impossibility, the next best thing is to know about him, for it is written that, "Of all human knowledge, that which is the greatest is to know the life of Jesus and how he lived it."

To see how Jesus personally touched and transformed the

lives of so many, let's step back some twenty centuries and visit the places Jesus went and meet the people Jesus met. Let's follow Jesus through fourteen major events of his earthly ministry.

Walter Ziglar

# Day 1:

# The Ordination Sermon

*"Sermon on the Mount"*

*(January 12, AD 27)*

# The Ordination Sermon
"Sermon on the Mount"
Sunday, January 12, AD 27

*Their message to the world as Jesus would soon tell his Apostles was: "Seek first the Kingdom of God and his righteousness, and all things shall be added to you." (Matthew 6:33, Luke 12:31)*

I t was approaching noon this beautiful Sunday in early January when Jesus called the twelve apostles together for their ordination as public preachers of the gospel of the kingdom.

Anticipating their call any day, the apostles were in reasonable proximity to one another, fishing by the shores of Lake Capernaum. Thus it was easy for Jesus to gather them up "two by two" for the short journey to the highlands north of Capernaum where he proceeded to instruct them in preparation for their formal ordination.

Who were these hearty Galileans so willing to give up their vocations and, for some, to follow a complete stranger?

Back in February of AD 26 Jesus came down from the hills to meet with the followers of John the Baptist who were encamped at Pella. Here Jesus would choose his first apostles.

Of all John's followers, one named Andrew was the most

profoundly impressed with Jesus. Andrew and his younger brother, Simon (Peter), had known Jesus for some time by virtue of their association with James and John Zebedee, in whose father's boat factory he had labored as a carpenter.

Of the twelve apostles, these four men would remain closest to the Master and would be chosen to accompany him at all times, except when he was off by himself communing with the Father.

Andrew had been an admirer of Jesus for some time and when asked by Jesus to join in the service of discipleship he readily accepted. Of all his associates, Andrew was the best judge of men and, having been recognized by the twelve as a superb administrator, he would soon be designated chairman and director general of the apostles. As the head of the apostolic group, Andrew had to remain on duty with his brethren, missing on a number of occasions the close intimate association with Jesus, which his brother, Simon, and the Zebedee brothers enjoyed.

Andrew was a mild-mannered man of superb character, possessing clear insight, logical thought and great personal stability. Although Andrew did not possess the fiery rhetoric of his younger brother, he was not impetuous and was far more even-tempered than Simon Peter.

They then sought out Simon who was welcomed by Jesus as his second apostle. Simon Peter, a full three years younger than Andrew, was a supreme optimist, but also a man of impulse, inclined to strong feelings. Peter was a natural and inspirational leader of men, a quick thinker and fluent speaker, but not a deep reasoner. All too often he would speak without thinking and act on impulse. Nevertheless, this impetuous young soul did more in one generation than any other one man, aside from Paul, to establish the kingdom and send its messengers to the four corners of the earth.

James and John, who had just come down from the hills after looking for Jesus, felt somewhat slighted at not being called first, having known him longer, but Jesus told them that they were already with him in the spirit of the kingdom, even before their fishing partners had made requests to be received.

James, the older of the two apostle sons of Zebedee, was a man of strong emotions. He had a fiery temper when his righteous indignation was aroused, but aside from periodic outbursts of anger, his temperament was much like that of Andrew. And like Andrew, James possessed an ability to see all sides of a proposition. Next to Peter, he was the best public orator of the twelve. It was because of his persuasive abilities to attract the multitudes to the kingdom that Herod Agrippa, grandson of Herod the Great, feared him the most. He was a vigorous individual, but never impulsive, providing an excellent balance wheel for Peter in the years to come.

John, his younger brother, was more quiet and introspective, but inordinately intolerant. John, more than James, wanted to call down fire from heaven on the heads of the disrespectful Samaritans, and when, on occasion, he would encounter strangers teaching in Jesus' name, he would rebuke them. But John possessed many superb traits of personality, one of which was his cool and daring courage. He was the one apostle who followed right along with Jesus the night of his arrest and dared to accompany his Master even at great personal peril right up to the crucifixion. Thoroughly dependable, he would become closely associated with Peter and become his right hand support on the day of Pentecost.

John would become a strong supporter of the church at Jerusalem and, because of this, he would be imprisoned several times and banished to the Isle of Patmos by the emperor, Domitian, for a period of four years until the new emperor, Nerva, came to power in Rome.

It was these four apostles, Andrew, Peter, James and John, who met with John the Baptist that evening to discuss Jesus' plan and who duly parted the next morning for Galilee.

As they headed for Galilee they crossed the Jordan, going by way of Nain to Nazareth. Along the roadside they met up with Philip and his friend, Nathaniel, who were on their way to Pella to hear more from John about the coming of the kingdom of God. Philip was a commonplace, matter-of-fact individual and if he had any weakness it was his great lack of imagination; he was always wanting to be shown. This lack of imagination was affected by his methodical thoroughness, as he was both mathematical and systematic. Because of these characteristics he would be made the steward of the apostles, and a good one at that. But for the most part, there was little about Philip's personality that was impressive. He was usually referred to as "Philip of Bethsaida, the town where Andrew and Peter lived." Philip was never easily discouraged; he was a plodder with a rare gift of getting others to come and see for themselves. He was most effective, when confronted by skeptics in his subsequent teaching, by simply saying, "Come and see," and this is precisely what he said to Nathaniel, ben Bartholomew his first convert.

Although Philip had known Jesus and the four, having himself lived in Bethsaida, he was unsure as to whom to follow until Jesus said, *Follow me.* (John 1:43)

Philip was thrilled with the assurance that he had found the deliverer and hurried over to Nathaniel who had been reclining under a fig tree, commenting, *We have found him of whom Moses and the prophets wrote, Jesus of Nazareth, the son of Joseph.* (John 1:45) Now Nathaniel was from Cana and, having only heard of Jesus, he responded by saying, *Can any good thing come out of Nazareth?* But Philip, taking him by the arm, said, *Come and see.* (John 1:46)

As they walked towards him, Jesus spoke, *Behold an Israelite indeed in whom there is no deceit.* (John 1:47) And Nathaniel knew immediately that Jesus was the Son of God. Nathaniel, the second youngest of the apostles next to John, possessed a number of virtues; among them was his honesty and sincerity. If there was any flaw in his character it was an inordinate amount of pride. He would sometimes go to extremes with his personal prejudices. Even before he met Jesus he would say, "Can anything good come out of Nazareth?" But Nathaniel also possessed a great sense of humor and he was greatly loved by all of his brethren. Although Nathaniel seldom took himself seriously, he progressively took his apostleship more seriously. And this philosophic poet and humorist would perform his duty of looking after the families of the twelve with consummate care.

Jesus and the apostles journeyed to Capernaum where Jesus worked in the Zebedee boat shop while instructing the six for a period of four months.

It was not until he received news of John's arrest that he laid down his tools and proclaimed, *The kingdom of God is at hand.* (Matthew 4:12, 17, Mark 1:14, 15)

On Sunday, June 23, Jesus imparted his final instructions to the six, directing them to go forth two by two teaching the glad tidings of the kingdom. They were also given the task of choosing six new apostle candidates for presentation to Jesus.

Each of the six was to choose one, and these new apostles were:

Matthew Levi, the customs collector of Capernaum, who maintained his office just east of the city near the borders of Batanea. He was chosen by Andrew.

Thomas Didymus, chosen by Philip, was a former carpenter and stone mason of Gadara and more recently a fisherman from Tarichea.

James Alpheus, a fisherman from Kheresa, was picked by James Zebedee.

Judas Alpheus, the twin brother of James, was selected by John Zebedee. He was also a fisherman.

Simon Zelotes, chosen by Peter, had been a merchant, and was currently a high officer in a Jewish patriotic organization of the Zealots.

Judas Iscariot, selected by Nathaniel, was the son of wealthy Jewish parents living in Jericho, and had been disowned by his Sadducee parents for following John the Baptist. He was the only Judean among the twelve.

Jesus reviewed the list and the next day he and the six went to call upon Matthew, the customs collector. Matthew was waiting for them at the toll house and when Jesus approached, saying, *Follow me,* (Matthew 9:9) he arose and went to his home with Jesus and the apostles. Matthew was a man of modest wealth, having earned his living as a tax gatherer (publican). Although short-sighted and materialistic at times, this loyal apostle was wholeheartedly devoted to the cause and over the years would give away every cent of his personal wealth, as it became his duty to keep the apostolic treasury replenished. Although a good businessman, upon joining the apostles, his only business became that of finding God. Matthew did all his personal work in a quiet and personal way, and when funds were low he never thought twice to draw upon his own personal resources. Possibly this loyal and dedicated apostle gave so much of his personal assets in order to make amends for his past, but whether or not this was the reason, he grew to love his brethren and did everything he could to provide for their comfort, and they genuinely loved him.

After lunching at Matthew's house, Jesus and the seven now headed for Simon Zelotes' place of business where Jesus again said, *Follow me.* Simon Zelotes was a rabid revolutionist, a *fearless firebrand of agitation* who eventually became a powerful and effective preacher of *peace on earth and good will among men.* Simon was a dynamo; he was born to argue, and when it came to dealing with the legalistic minds of the educated Jews, Simon the debater, was well equipped to deal with them. He was a man of intense loyalties and warm personal devotions and he loved Jesus. They all returned to Matthew's house where the Levi family had prepared a reception banquet for Jesus.

It was the custom in those days for all interested persons to linger about the banquet room observing the guest and men of honor as they engaged in conversation.

As the dinner progressed, the joys of the evening increased and everybody had a good time, except for the onlooking Pharisees who could only condemn Jesus in their hearts for participating in such lighthearted merriment.

*Why do you eat and drink with publicans and sinners?* they demanded. (Luke 5:30)

And Jesus spoke to them saying, *To you who stand about criticizing me in your hearts because I have come here to make merry with these friends, let me say that I have come to proclaim joy to the socially downtrodden and spiritual liberty to the moral captives. Need I remind you that it is not those who are well that need a physician but those who are sick. I have come not to call the righteous, but sinners.* (Luke 5:31-32)

The next morning, Jesus and the eight went over to the Kheresa to call on James and Judas Alpheus, the fishermen. Once again Jesus said, "Follow me," and the brothers did just that. James and Judas Alpheus were the twin sons of Mary, one of the five women to visit the tomb of Jesus. These two lovable brothers had neither strong points nor weak points. They were not of a philosophical bent, nor did they enter into theological debates in winning souls for the kingdom. They, more than the others, came from the "common folk," whom they attracted. Although far from dynamic, they quietly assisted their brethren in the "little things," such as attending the camp and preparing the food. Although they were simple in mind, they were big of heart, kind and generous. They were nicknamed affectionately by their fellow apostles, Thadeus and Lebbaeus. After spending the evening at the Alpheus' home, Jesus and the ten set out the next morning for Tarichea by boat.

The last to be called were Thomas and Judas who were waiting for Jesus and the ten at the landing docks at Tarichea.

Philip and Nathaniel presented their respective nominees to Jesus and upon greeting them he said, "Follow me." Thomas was the real scientist of the twelve, possessing a truly analytical mind. Nevertheless he was a natural born fault-finder — a real pessimist. Some days Thomas would be blue and downcast, which may have stemmed from his youth when he lost his twin sister. Sometimes he would become so despondent as to go away for a day or two. But Thomas was not a man to stay down. When he came out of his depression he would bounce back as a man who had doubts, faced them, and overcame them. When it was time to move ahead Thomas was always the first to say, "Let's go."

Judas Iscariot was a man beset by divided loyalties. In his heart he might have loved Jesus, but his mind overruled his heart; it was this conflict between mind and soul that eventually led to his betrayal of the Master and his subsequent suicide. As a child, he was spoiled, pampered, and petted and eventually developed exaggerated ideas about his self-importance. He harbored vengeance against those whom he thought had mistreated him. He was, for the most part, an embittered human being and when he finally came to the realization that Jesus was not to fill the shoes of the Jewish Messiah, he allowed the dictates of a proud and vengeful mind to swiftly plunge him down into confusion, despair and destruction.

After refreshing themselves, Jesus took the twelve apart for a season of instruction. These apostles were soon to learn that Jesus had come to proclaim a new gospel of salvation and to establish a new way of finding God.

Some of these teachings would prove quite foreign to them, such as preaching forgiveness of sin through faith without penance or sacrifice, and that the Father in heaven loves all his children with the same eternal love.

There would be five months of testing and instruction before the apostles would be ordained in January of the following year. This was a relatively quiet period for the twelve as they would alternate between instruction and fishing in order to provide for their respective families. Most of them were married and some had several children, therefore, during this period the apostles had to make arrangements for the support of their families so as not to worry about their financial welfare during their period of public ministry.

17

During this season of work and study, the apostles would learn that the Master had a profound respect for every human being he encountered, that the individual came before anything else. And this included women, as Jesus made it very clear to them that women were to be accorded equal rights with men in the kingdom. The apostles were not accustomed to such liberal treatment of women, but this was only one of many adjustments they would make over the next five months.

During these five months, the apostles carried out their personal work in Capernaum, Bethsaida-Julias, Chorazin, Gerasa, Hippos, Magdala, Cana, Bethlehem, Jotapata, Ramah, Safed, Gischalda, Gadara and Abila.

It was during these travels that the apostles came in contact with various religious groups and political parties of Palestine.

One of these groups was the Sadducees, which consisted of the priesthood and certainly wealthy Jews. Pragmatic in politics, these aristocrats were the dominant party of the senate of Sanhedrin and maintained control until the destruction of Jerusalem in AD 70. They were not as concerned with adhering to the letter of the law as were the Pharisees, and refused to accept the authority of the legal rulings of the scholars of the Hasidim.

The other major religious party was the Pharisees, made up of scribes and rabbis, often referring to themselves as the "associates." Having adopted many teachings not clearly found in Hebrew Scriptures, they were considered the more progressive group among the Jews. One of their teachings concerned belief in the resurrection of the dead, a doctrine only maintained by a later prophet, Daniel.

The Pharisees were the teachers and the interpreters of the law, developing binding oral tradition handed down from master to disciple. And it was this devotion to learning, to scholarship and to the Torah that differentiated the Pharisees from the priestly nobility of the Sadducees who preferred life to be lived in the here and now.

Another group was the Essenes, which was a truly religious sect as opposed to a religious party. This sect originated in the Maccabean revolt and lived as a brotherhood in monasteries, had all things in common, and refrained from marriage. They specialized in teachings about angels.

All but angels were the Zealots, a group of intense Jewish patriots, who advocated that any and all methods were justified in the overthrow of the Roman yoke.

A purely political party which advocated emancipation from direct Roman rule by a restoration of the Herodian dynasty were the Herodians.

Intermingled among these various groups were the Samaritans with whom "the Jews had no dealings," although they held many similar ideas on Jewish teachings.

All of these parties and sects had one thing in common; they all believed in the sometime coming of the Messiah — a national deliverer. But Jesus made it clear to these groups that his mission was not to fulfill the role as the son of David. He had not come to restore Jewish political might. He would teach his apostles to proclaim the "good tidings of the kingdom of heaven." He would impress upon these men that they must "show forth love, compassion and sympathy." These apostles were taught that the kingdom of heaven was a spiritual experience having to do with the enthronement of God in the hearts of men.

These apostles were to learn from Jesus that in the kingdom of heaven there shall neither be Jew nor Gentile, only those who seek perfection through service and that those who would be great in the Father's kingdom must first become the server of all. (Matthew 20:26-27, Mark 10:43-44)

These were but some of the truths Jesus would teach the twelve prior to their becoming ambassadors of the kingdom. Now it was time for their ordination as public preachers of the gospel of the kingdom and they were ready and eager to represent the Master in proclaiming these truths.

Their message would be a simple one — seek first the kingdom of God and his righteousness, and in finding these, all other things essential to eternal survival shall be added to you. (Matthew 6:33, Luke 12:31)

They were to tell the people that this new kingdom shall consist not in the strength of armies nor in the might of riches, but rather in the glory of the divine spirit that shall come to teach the minds and rule the hearts of those who are reborn into this kingdom. This new kingdom is a brotherhood of love wherein righteousness reigns and is the desire of the good men of all ages, the hope of all the earth, and the fulfillment of the wise promises of all the prophets.

Peace on earth and good will to all men, they were to proclaim.

A gentle breeze prevailed on this clear and crisp winter morning as the apostles gathered before Jesus to hear his ordination sermon.

Kneeling about him in a circle, the Master placed his hands upon the head of each and prayed for them. *Even now that the kingdom is at hand, some of you will not die until you have seen the reign of God come in great power.* (Matthew 16:28, Mark 9:1, Luke 9:27)

These twelve were about to be ordained to go forth to proclaim liberty to the spiritual captives, joy to those in the bondage of fear, and to heal the sick in accordance with the Father's will, in the Son's name.

*When you find my children in distress, speak encouragingly to them saying:*

*Happy are the poor in spirit (the humble) for theirs is the treasure of the kingdom of heaven.* (Matthew 5:3, Mark 6:20) In Jesus' time and since, happiness has all too often been associated with material comfort, the result of accumulated wealth. In the story of the Pharisee and the publican praying in the temple, the one felt rich in spirit — egotistical, the other felt "poor in spirit" — humble; and it is the poor in spirit who seek for goals of spiritual wealth — for God. They are the ones who find the kingdom of heaven in their own hearts, and their happiness is achieved immediately. It was not the self-sufficient that Jesus had come to teach but the humble of spirit — the truth seeker.

*Happy are they who hunger and thirst for righteousness, for they shall be filled.* (Matthew 5:6) Again Jesus was telling his apostles that only those who felt poor in spirit would ever hunger for righteousness. It is only the humble who seek God's way and are willing to subordinate their will to God's leading. This righteousness of Jesus was a dynamic love, a fatherly-brotherly affection as exemplified in his commandment, "Love one another as I have loved you." It was not a negative self-righteousness or a thou-shalt-not type of righteousness; for how could one ever hunger for something negative — something not to do?

*Happy are the meek, for they shall inherit the earth.* (Matthew 5:5) This meekness Jesus was referring to was an attitude, that of man cooperating with God — *Your will be done.* And Jesus was the ideal of meekness for he always acted in accordance with the Father's will. (John 5:30)

**20**

*Happy are the pure in heart, for they shall see God.* (Matthew 5:8) Here Jesus was telling the apostles that it is the possessor of spiritual purity who comes to know God, not those who harbor envy, suspicion, hate and revenge. The pure in heart must learn to forgive and to love, even his enemies. Always did he admonish them: *Be you perfect, even as your Father in heaven is perfect.* (Matthew 5:48)

*Happy are they who mourn, for they shall be comforted.* (Matthew 5:4) Jesus was not referring to outward mourning but of inward mourning — man's tenderheartedness — his sensitivity and responsiveness to human need which creates genuine and lasting happiness. Such an attitude of human kindness safeguards the soul from the destructive influence of anger, hate and suspicion.

*Happy are the merciful, for they shall obtain mercy.* (Matthew 5:7) Jesus had long taught that in order to receive mercy one had to show mercy. These apostles were told to teach forgiveness, for true mercy is loving kindness, that which emanates from the trust of friendships. In order to be forgiven we must first learn to forgive; for it is only from a pure heart that we can obtain God's mercy.

*Happy are the peacemakers, for they shall be called the sons of God.* (Matthew 5:9) Although many of Jesus' followers were longing for a Messiah who would advocate a military deliverance from the yoke of Roman rule, Jesus had told them he did not come for that purpose; that he had come to reveal the Father's love which would come to rule the hearts of men. He was a peacemaker, but Jesus' peace was not of the passive or negative kind. It was a positive peacemaking which cures distrust and suspicion, not to be confused with peacemaking through fear and intimidation. *Let not your heart be troubled, neither let it be afraid* (John 14:27), he would tell his followers. Personal peace integrates personality and prevents ruinous conflicts. Social peace prevents fear, greed and anger, while political peace prevents racial hatred, national mistrust, and war. His teachings might be reflected in today's popular slogan, "Make peace, not war," by coming to know our neighbors through care and understanding and love rather than through fear and suspicion, and mistrust.

*Happy are they who are persecuted for righteousness' sake, for theirs is the kingdom of heaven.* (Matthew 5:10)

21

*Happy are you when men shall revile you and persecute you and shall say all manner of evil against you falsely. Rejoice and be exceedingly glad, for great is your reward in heaven.* (Matthew 5:11-12)

*Greater love has no man than to lay down his life for his friends,* Jesus would tell his apostles. (John 15:13) Jesus was the ultimate example of a man who was persecuted for right-eousness sake by a self-deceived few who felt threatened by his ministry of love and service. Our lesson should be his example of taking up the cross as a manifestation of his love for us while fully forgiving his enemies.

There can be no greater test of man than to hold steadfast through all manners of persecution and to be able to rejoice in the process while forgiving those who speak falsely against you. It is truly a badge of courage and a mark of greatness. For nothing is greater than returning good for evil — doing good in retaliation for injustice.

These are the Beatitudes of the Sermon on the Mount which Jesus gave his apostles based on faith and love, and not on law-ethics and duty.

Upon returning from the highlands north of Capernaum, Jesus and the twelve headed for the Zebedee home where they partook of a simple meal.

Later that evening, Jesus gathered the apostles around him in the Zebedee garden for further instruction.

He told them that the new gospel of the kingdom could not conform to that which is, but that nevertheless he had not come to set aside the law and the prophets. *I have not come to destroy but to fulfill, to enlarge and illuminate,* he told them. (Matthew 5:17) He came not to transgress the law but rather to write these new commandments on the tablets of their hearts.

And then he said, *Unless your righteousness surpasses that of the scribes and Pharisees, you shall not enter the kingdom of heaven.* (Matthew 5:20) To be sure, the scribes and Pharisees were moral men to the point of self-righteousness. The Master knew, however, that no man could make himself pure by merely obeying the law. A good disciple had to be right, not only in living but in his motives, for the only thing that exceeds right doing is right being. Thus, the characteristic of a good disciple was not that he did good things, but that he was good in motive because he had been made good by the supernatural grace of God.

Therefore, the righteousness of these apostles was to consist in love, mercy, and truth, and to be predicated upon the sincere desire to do the will of the heavenly Father.

And he further instructed them, *You have heard it said by those who teach the law: 'You shall not kill; that whosoever kills shall be subject to judgments.' I declare to you that everyone who is angry with his brother is in danger of condemnation.* (Matthew 5:21-22)

These apostles were learning that he who nurses hatred in his heart and plans vengeance in his mind stands in danger of judgment, for they must judge their fellows by their deeds as the Father in heaven judges by the intent.

*You have heard the teachers of the law say, 'You shall not commit adultery.' But I say to you that every man who looks upon a woman with intent to lust after her has already committed adultery with her in his heart.* (Matthew 5:27-28) Again they were learning that although they can only judge men by their acts, the Father in heaven looks into the hearts of his children and in mercy adjudges them in accordance with their interest and real desires.

The apostles were beginning to recognize the two viewpoints of all mortal conduct — the human and the divine; the ways of the flesh and the way of the spirit; the estimate of time and the viewpoint of eternity. It was difficult for these Galileans to shed their preconceived ideas of a Messiah on the order of David in favor of a spiritual kingdom in the hearts of men. But these teachings were of real value to them in the months to come.

Jesus went on to say, *And you must remember that I have sheep not of this flock, and that I am beholden to them also, and they will heed my voice; and there will be one flock with one shepherd.* (John 10:16)

Then Nathaniel asked, "Master, shall we give no place to justice? The law of Moses says, 'An eye for an eye, and a tooth for a tooth.' What shall we say?" And Jesus answered, *Do not resist him who is evil, but whoever slaps you on the right cheek, turn him the other also. And if anyone wants to sue you, and take your shirt, let him have your coat also. And whoever shall force you to go one mile, go with him two.* (Matthew 5:38-42)

The lesson was simple; although they were to practice

**23**

non-resistance, the apostles were not to passively submit to wrongdoing. Instead, they were to attempt to control a situation by acting in a positive fashion; they were to return good for evil.

These men were learning that measure for measure shall not be their rule, that the rulers of men may have such laws, but not so in the kingdom. Mercy was to determine their judgments and love their conduct, Jesus instructed them. He never ceased to warn his disciples against the evil practice of retaliation; he made no allowance for revenge, the idea of getting even. He deplored the holding of grudges. He disallowed the idea of an eye for an eye and a tooth for a tooth. Do not make the mistake of fighting evil with its own weapons as a wrong is never righted by vengeance, the apostles would learn.

*Do your good deeds in secret,* Jesus told them. *When you give alms, let not the left hand know what the right hand does. And when you pray, go apart by yourselves and use not vain repetitions and meaningless phrases. Always remember that the Father knows what you need even before you ask him.* (Matthew 6:2-8) And *be not given to fasting with a sad countenance to be seen by men.* (Matthew 6:16) And *lay not up for yourselves treasures on earth, but by your unselfish service lay up for yourselves treasures in heaven, for where your treasures are, there will your hearts be also.* (Matthew 6:19-21)

*The lamp of the body is the eye; if therefore, your eye is generous, your whole body will be full of light. But if your eye is selfish, the whole body will be filled with darkness!* (Matthew 6:22-23, Luke 11:34)

And then Jesus instructed the apostles on divided allegiance. No man can serve two masters. You cannot serve God and mammon. Having now enlisted unreservedly in the work of the kingdom, be not anxious for your lives; much less be concerned with what you shall eat or what you shall drink; nor yet for your bodies, what clothing you shall wear. Already have you learned that willing hands and earnest hearts shall not go hungry. And now when you prepare to devote all your energies to the work of the kingdom, be assured that the Father will not be unmindful of your needs. Seek first the kingdom of God and when you have found entrance thereto, all things needful shall be added to you. *Therefore, be not unduly anxious for the morrow. Tomorrow will take care of itself.* (Matthew 6:24-34, Luke 12-23)

*My brethren, as I send you forth you are the salt of the earth, salt with a saving savor. But if this salt has lost its savor, wherewith shall it be salted? It is henceforth good for nothing but to be cast out and trodden underfoot of men.* (Matthew 5:13, Mark 9:50, Luke 14:34-35)

It was quite a compliment for these men to be called the salt of the earth as salt in Jesus' day was a precious commodity. It was not only used as a preservative, it was used to flavor food and as a means of barter — money. The word salary is derived from salt. Jesus was telling his apostles that as long as their message was true it had flavor value, but if the truth of his teachings was distorted or crystallized into rigid doctrine, it would lose its flavor and have little worth and would eventually become static and die.

The Master continued, *You are the light of the world. A city set on a hill cannot be hid. Neither do men light a candle and put it under a bushel, but on a candlestick; and it gives light to all who are in the house. Let your light so shine before men that they may see your good works and be led to glorify your Father who is in heaven.* (Matthew 5:14-16, Luke 11:33-36)

The apostles were beginning to realize that soon they would be center stage and that Jesus was telling them their message was to be positive, requiring action — service in the human brotherhood. It was not to be a message grounded in negative postulates — thou shalt not — nor was their light to be blinding in laws and dogmas so as to confuse and frustrate.

In effect, Jesus was telling the apostles that their light should not attract attention to oneself but at the same time it should shine so as to guide their fellows into new and godly paths of enhanced living; that strong characters are not derived from not doing wrong but rather from actually doing right; that happy and effective people are motivated not by fear of wrong doing but by the love of right doing.

The gospel of the kingdom was slowly beginning to sink in with these fearless and adventurous twelve. Unselfish service in the human brotherhood in accordance with the Father's will was the goal of man, as "Unselfishness is the badge of human greatness."

Said the Master, *You have heard it said, 'You shall love your neighbor and hate your enemy,' but I say to you: Love your enemies, do good to those who hate you, bless those who curse you, and pray for those who despitefully use you. And whatsoever you believe that men should to you, do you also to them.* (Matthew 5:44, 7:14, Luke 6:27-28, 31, 35)

*Your Father in heaven makes the sun to shine on the evil as well as upon the good; likewise he sends rain on the just and the unjust.* (Matthew 5:45) *Be merciful even as God is merciful and you shall be perfect, even as your heavenly Father is perfect.* (Matthew 5:48, Luke 6:36) *You are commissioned to save men not to judge them. Therefore, do not judge lest you be judged. For in this way you judge, you will be judged; and by your standard of measure it shall be measured to you. Make not the mistake of trying to pluck a mote out of your brother's eye when there is a beam in your own eye. Having first cast the beam out of your own eye, you can better see to cast the mote out of your brother's eye.* (Matthew 7:1-5, Luke 6:41-42)

*You have heard it said, 'If the blind lead the blind, they both shall fall into the pit.' If you would but guide others into the kingdom, you must yourselves walk in the clear light of living truth.* (Luke 6:39) *Present not that which is holy to dogs, neither cast your pearls before swine lest they trample your gems under-foot and turn to rend you.* (Matthew 7:6)

*I warn you against false prophets who will come to you in sheep's clothing but inwardly are ravenous wolves. By their fruits you shall know them. Do men gather grapes from thorns or figs from thistles? Even so every good tree brings forth good fruit, but the corrupt tree bears evil fruit. A good tree cannot yield evil fruit, neither can a corrupt tree produce good fruit. Every tree that does not bring forth good fruit is presently hewn down and cast into the fire. So then you will know them by their fruits.* (Matthew 7:15-20, Luke 3:8-9, John 15:2, 5-8)

In gaining an entrance into the kingdom of heaven, it is the motive that counts. The Father looks into the hearts of men and judges by their inner longings and their sincere intentions, Jesus was telling them. The Master was instructing them that moral worth cannot be derived from mere repression, by obeying the injunction, "Thou shall not," as fear and shame are unworthy motivations for religious living. Their tree instead, was to be one of love and service which would certainly bear fruit; for the only valid religion is one that reveals the fatherhood of God and enhances the brotherhood of man.

No longer were they to concern themselves with religious

negativism, for those trees could bear no fruit, and the tree which bears no fruit is, "hewn down and cast into the fire."

Their gospel was to produce a lasting spiritual fruit, fruit that would be as fresh in their day as 2,000 years from then. *You did not choose me, but I chose you and appointed you that you should go and bear fruit and that your fruit should remain, that whatever you ask of the Father in my name he may give to you.* (John 15:16)

And then ending this discussion Jesus said to the twelve, *In the great day of the kingdom judgment, many will say to me, 'Did we not prophesy in your name and by your name do many wonderful works?' but I will be compelled to say to them, 'I never knew you; depart from me you who are false teachers.' But everyone who hears this charge and sincerely executes his commission to represent me before man even as I have represented my Father to you, I will liken him unto a wise man, who builds his house upon a rock.* (Matthew 7:21-24)

It was now late in the evening; it had been a very long day so Jesus bid his apostles a good night. Exhausted, many of them fell asleep by the warm fire in the garden.

*Day 2:*

# **D**iscourse at Jotapata

*(January 13 to February 6, AD 28)*

# Discourse at Jotapata

9 Day Period
January 13 — January 22, AD 28

**Tuesday, January 13:** *Apostolic party arrives in Capernaum from Pella Camp (distance: 30 miles). Headquartered at Zebedee home in Bethsaida.*

**Thursday, January 15:** *Depart Capernaum for Jotapata via the small town of Rimmon (distance: 20 miles).*

**Sunday, January 18:** *Leave Rimmon for Jotapata (distance: 3 miles). Start of Preaching tour. Judge not that you be not judged. (Matt. 7:1) Love your enemies; pray for those who persecute you. (Matt. 5:44)*

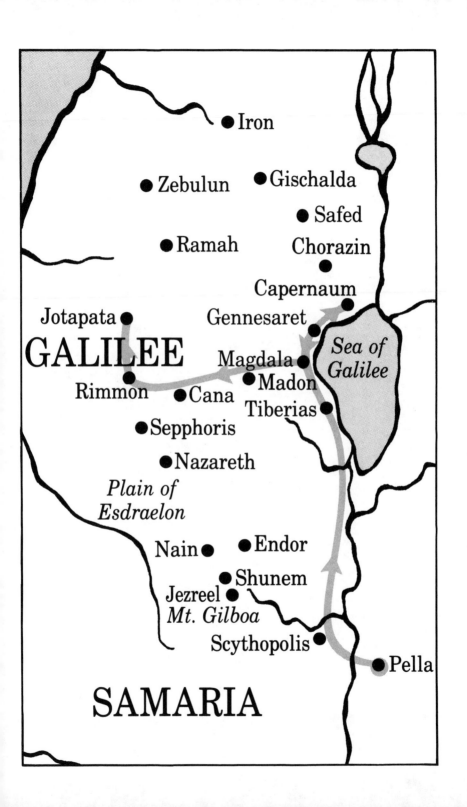

One week before Jesus and the apostolic group started on their first preaching tour of the cities of Galilee, John the Baptist was executed by order of Herod Antipas the evening of January 10, AD 28.

The next day several of John's disciples who were tarrying in Machaerus heard of his execution and petitioned Herod for John's body which they buried at Sebaste, the home of Abner, one of John's followers and later founder of the eastern church at Philadelphia.

The following day, John's followers headed north to meet up with Jesus and his apostles at Pella.

Early the morning of January 13, Jesus and the apostles, accompanied by several dozen disciples, made their way to Capernaum where they lodged at the Zebedee home in Bethsaida. It was here Jesus made plans to launch his first public preaching tour of Galilee.

In the first century AD, the vast majority of people in Galilee lived in rural villages where farming and fishing were the major industries.

Capernaum, located on the northwestern shore of the Sea of Galilee, was the area's major town, typically made up of fishermen, farmers and small merchants. It was near the border between Herod Antipas' territory and the region to the east controlled by his brother, Herod Philip.

The whole countryside of Galilee was made up of lush and fertile valleys. The majority of its inhabitants were Jews, but a number of Gentiles, both slave and free, lived among them. Among the Gentiles were Syrians who migrated from the north and Greeks who moved east after the conquest of the region by Alexander the Great. The Romans settled sometime later, in the middle of the first century.

Comparatively speaking, the Jews were smaller in stature, most of whom, in keeping with tradition, wore beards. They wore their hair long, as did the women, and their skin was deeply tanned, a result of a lifetime spent out-of-doors.

The Galileans spoke a provincial dialect of Aramaic which to their Jerusalem brethren was crude, at best. These hearty, country people were not only considered uncultured and unsophisticated, they were also distrusted by the Jerusalem leaders, suspecting them of being too liberal in their observance of the law.

Galilean social life centered on the family, most of which were large, close knit and hard working. The husband was the spiritual and legal head of the household, as well as the final arbiter of all issues dealing with the welfare of his family.

The laws were strict and all village Jews were governed by the same stringent system of moral, religious and social codes. It was a society of rituals, each Jew reciting a blessing for nearly every occasion, including waking up, dressing, lacing their sandals and washing their hands.

No wonder these hard working, country folk, who were somewhat lax on ritual, seemed suspect to the more sophisticated Jerusalemites, who insisted upon strict adherence to the laws of the elders.

Home life offered little in the way of material comfort. Except for the wealthy households, there was little in the way of furniture. The house itself, unlike the stone houses of the larger cities, was usually made of mud brick, consisting of just one or two all purpose rooms.

Bedding was all but non-existent. Family members usually stretched out on mats covering themselves with tunics and cloaks. There was no bathroom, as the communal courtyard provided the toilet, the well and the washing basin. The roof of the house was usually flat, making it an ideal sleeping area during the hot summer months. The doorways were usually narrow and low, forcing a man to bend slightly upon entering.

Although Jesus and his apostles usually ate three meals a day, it was customary for most Jewish families to eat just twice a day. Breakfast was usually a light meal carried to the field and eaten by mid-morning, while suppers, in contrast, were very substantial, consisting of vegetables, eggs, bread, cheese, butter, nuts, fruit and wine, served, perhaps, with fish or fowl. Red meat, usually a rarity, was only served on special occasions when a fatted calf or lamb might be sacrificed and ritually bled before cooking.

Farming meant everything to the rural Jew; only God and family were more important. Land ownership, by tradition, was a matter of family inheritance, dating back to the times Joshua distributed conquered lands to the tribes of Israel. By the time of Jesus, the best properties were owned and controlled by relatively few landowners — mainly the rulers of Rome, the Herodian family, and the priestly aristocracy. On these lands the farmers may well have been tenants or slaves.

Soil was chiefly composed of Mediterranean brown, or terra rosa, a residue of dissolving limestone.

Most Galileans grew a variety of crops, making their families all but self-sufficient. Since the Galilean farmer was so tied to his land, his work was determined by the seasons, and the beginning or ending of these agricultural seasons was cause for ritual celebration.

To mark the end of the grain harvest, the farmers and their families celebrated *Shavuot,* or the Festival of Weeks, which always fell on the day following the completion of seven weeks after the start of Passover. Also known as Pentecost (from the Greek word meaning 50th day), this feast commemorated the revelation of Mount Sinai when, according to the book of Exodus, God gave to Moses the Ten Commandments. This was the same day Jesus would eventually proclaim to his followers that they would receive the "Spirit of Truth."

Another celebration held in conjunction with the final harvest was the feast of Succoth (also known as the Feast of Booths or Tabernacles) referring to the open booths or huts the farmers lived in during the annual grape and olive harvest. This season of thanksgiving was by far the most joyous time of the year and generally included a trip to the Temple in Jerusalem.

Aside from those who made their living through agriculture or fishing, most villages supported a number of independent craftsmen, including carpenters, blacksmiths, tanners, porters, dyers, mat makers, leather workers and basket weavers.

It was to these simple Galileans and their humble villages that Jesus would conduct his first preaching tour.

The next few days were spent by Jesus at the Zebedee house, instructing his apostles preparatory to the first open and public tour.

The home of James and John Zebedee was a common gathering place for the Master and his apostles as their parents were very fond of Jesus; and it was at their boat shop, the largest on Lake Capernaum, that Jesus worked as a carpenter. This factory was known throughout the countryside for its exquisite workmanship and superior boats.

David Zebedee, James' and John's elder brother, was a silent worker for the apostolic group, providing an extensive communications network that kept the families apprised of the apostles' whereabouts.

On the Sabbath before their planned departure, Jesus spoke at the Capernaum synagogue. Not long after his afternoon sermon, he encountered a young man apparently possessed by an "unclean spirit." He was heard to say, *What have we to do with you, Jesus of Nazareth? You are the holy one of God; have you come to destroy us?* Jesus bade the people to be quiet and taking the young man by the hand said, *Come out of him.* He was immediately healed. (Mark 1:23-26; Luke 4:31-35)

After this remarkable healing, Jesus and his followers headed for the home of James and John Zebedee. Most of the cooking and the housework in the Zebedee home was done by Simon Peter's wife, and her mother, since Peter's home was just a short distance away.

On their way to the Zebedee home, Jesus and the apostles stopped off at Simon Peter's house to visit with Amatha, Peter's mother-in-law. She had been suffering from malarial fever and it was here Jesus ministered to her, healing her of fever and sickness. (Mark 1:30-31; Luke 4:38-39; Matthew 8:14-15)

By the time the apostolic party reached the Zebedee home, word of Jesus' healing the afflicted arrived to meet them.

As Jesus stepped from the porch, his eyes met hundreds of ailing human beings. Maneuvering closer to them his compassion for them became so great that they were all instantly healed, some several hundred of them. (Matthew 8:16; Mark 1:32-34; Luke 4:40)

This healing of so many at one time raised the apostles' spirits to their highest levels and this was probably the greatest day of all the great days of their association with Jesus.

They must have been thrilled by the vision of what was to come if this amazing manifestation of healing power was just the beginning.

It was on this high note that the apostolic party set out upon their journey to the cities of Galilee, a sojourn lasting two months, ending with their return to Capernaum in mid-March.

They would visit a number of cities including Rimmon, Jotapata, Ramah, Zebulun, Iron, Gischalda, Chorazin, Madon, Cana, Nain and Endor. These were the main cities in which they would tarry and preach while proclaiming the gospel of the kingdom as they passed through the smaller towns.

Having left the small city of Rimmon, once dedicated to the worship of a Babylonian God of the Air, Ramman, Jesus and his apostles headed for the small town of Jotapata.

This was the same Jotapata Josephus defended some 40 years later against Vespasian's seige. In that battle, Josephus, a young Jewish Zealot of 30, was commissioned to defend Galilee at its stronghold Jotapata. As the battle raged, only 40 Jewish soldiers remained alive, hiding with him in a cave. Josephus wished to surrender, but his men threatened to kill him if he tried. Since they preferred death to capture, he persuaded them to draw lots to fix the order in which each should die by the hand of the next. When all were dead but Josephus and one other, he induced him to surrender.

Eventually this young warrior became a useful advisor to Vespasian, who later became emperor.

It was in this small village of Jotapata that Jesus taught many truths, especially to his followers the second night of the tour, Monday, January 19, AD 28.

Much of this discussion had to do with man's reception to God's beckoning — man's willingness to be spirit led.

Jesus' followers well knew that conscious and persistent regard for iniquity in the heart of man gradually destroys the prayer connection of the human soul with the spirit circuits of communication between man and God.

These Jotapatans were told that God hears the petitions of his children, but that when the human heart deliberately and persistently harbors the concepts of evil and iniquity, communication with the Father becomes well-nigh impossible. And they were told, in order to keep open God's ever flowing stream of divine ministry, they must be forgiving of their fellow man. For Jesus said, *For if you forgive men their trespasses, your heavenly Father will also forgive you; but if you do not forgive men their trespasses, neither will your Father forgive your trespasses.* (Matthew 6:14; Mark 11:25-26)

These men well knew the Hebrew Scriptures that said, *I have called and you refused to hear; I stretched out my hand, but no man regarded. You have set at naught all my counsel, and you have rejected my reproof,* and because of this rebellious attitude it becomes inevitable that man shall call upon God and fail to receive an answer. Having rejected the way of life *you may seek me diligently in your times of suffering, but you will not find me.* (Proverbs 1:24-29)

The Master told them that, *They who would receive mercy must show mercy; judge not that you be not judged.* (Matthew 7:1-2; Luke 6:36-37)

These Jotopatans, remembering the proverb that states, *Who so stops his ears to the cry of the poor, he shall some day cry for help, and no one will hear him,* (Proverbs 21:13) were being told that the sincerity of any prayer is the assurance of its being heard. For Jesus told to them that when they have become wholly dedicated to the doing of the will of the Father in heaven, the answer to all their petitions will be forthcoming because these prayers will be in full accordance with the Father's will, and the Father's will is ever manifest throughout his vast universe. *Then whatsoever you shall ask the Father in my name, he will give it to you,* he told them. (John 14:13-14; 15:7; 16:23-24)

*Ask and it shall be given to you; seek and you shall find; knock and it shall be opened.* *For everyone who asks receives, and he who seeks finds, and to him who knocks it shall be opened.* (Matthew 7:7-8, Luke 11:9-10)

These men were learning that it is the motive of the prayer that gives way the divine ear, not the social, economic, or the apparent religious status of the one who prays. They were learned men in terms of Scripture and well knew those familiar passages from the Psalms which state, *Let your delight be of God, and he shall surely give you the sincere desires of your heart.* (Psalms 37:4-6) *Commit your way to the Lord; trust in him, and he will act.* (Psalms 37:5) *For the Lord hears the cry of the needy, and he will regard the prayer of the destitute.* (Psalms 102:17) *Create in me a clean heart, O God, and renew a right spirit within me.* (Psalms 51:10)

The thrust of the Master's sermon to his Jotapatan followers was not to become self-centered in their prayers; to avoid praying· too much for themselves but to pray more for the spiritual progress of their brethren; to avoid materialistic praying but instead pray in the spirit and for the abundance of the gifts of the spirit.

Jesus told them he had come from the Father. He would present their petitions in accordance with their real needs and desires, and in accordance with the Father's will if they asked in his name. (John 14:10, 14, 15:16, 16:23-24)

He went on to tell them, *Love your enemies, and pray for those who persecute you.* (Matthew 5:44, Luke 6:28)

They were told that prayer is a personal matter and to not let men hear their personal prayers.

*Let your real prayers always be in secret,* Jesus exclaimed. (Matthew 6:6)

They were told that God is spirit and that *those who worship him should worship in spirit and in truth.* (John 4:24)

And they were warned against thinking that their prayers would be rendered more efficacious by using meaningless repetitions, and eloquent phraseology as did the Gentiles. *Therefore,* said Jesus, *do not be like them; for your Father knows what you need before you ask him.* (Matthew 6:8)

Pray then in this way:
*Our Father who art in heaven,*

*Hallowed by thy name.*
*They kingdom come*
*Thy will be done*
*On earth as it is in heaven.*
*Give us this day our daily bread*
*And forgive us our debts*
*As we have forgiven our debtors*
*And lead us not into temptation,*
*But deliver us from evil.* (Matthew 6:9-13)

The whole group then read the Psalm that praises the Lord's goodness — Psalm 92. *It is a good thing to give thanks to the Lord and to sing praises to the name of the Most High, to acknowledge his loving kindness every morning and his faithfulness every night, for God has made me glad through his work. In everything I will give thanks according to the will of God.* (Psalm 92:1, 2, 4)

Then Jesus told his followers what Paul told the Philippians, to not be over anxious about their common needs. They should not be apprehensive concerning the problems of their earthly existence, and when praying, pray with the spirit of thanksgiving; let their needs be spread out before the Father who is in heaven. (Phil. 4:6)

As the crowd disbursed that early evening in mid-January, some were quoting Scripture such as Psalm 69 which says, *I will praise the name of God with a song and will magnify him with thanksgiving. And this will please the Lord better than the sacrifice of an ox or bullock with horns and hoofs.* (Psalms 69:30-31)

Others may have been reflecting on the message of Jesus concerning prayer and worship.

No matter their thoughts, they were all mightily moved by this inspiring message.

*Day 3:*

# ealing from a Distance

*(Late January to Mid-March AD 28)*

# Healing from a Distance
7 Week Period
Late January — Mid-March AD 28

**Thursday, January 22:** *Depart for Ramah (distance: 6 miles). "The Son is naturally endowed with the life of the Father." (John 5:26)*

**Friday, January 23:** *Depart for Zebulun (distance: 5 miles).*

**Sunday, January 25:** *Arrive in Iron (distance: 7 miles). Jesus heals the leper. (Matt. 8:1-3, Mark 1:40, Luke 5:12-13)*

**Thursday, January 29:** *Depart for Gischalda (distance: 5 miles).*

**Sunday, February 1:** *Depart for Chorazin (distance: 10 miles). Spent almost a week but won few believers in this town.*

**Friday, February 6:** *Depart for Capernaum (distance: 3 miles).*

**Sunday, February 8:** *Apostolic party departs Capernaum for Cana via the village of Madon (distance: 10 miles).*

**Tuesday, February 10:** *Arrive in the town of Cana. On Friday, Jesus heals the son of Titus, a prominent citizen of Capernaum (distance: 5 miles).*

**Friday, February 13:** *Depart for Nain (distance: 14 miles). Jesus raises the widow's son from the dead. (Luke 7:11-16)*

**Sunday, February 15:** *Depart for Endor (distance: 4 miles).*

**Tuesday, February 17:** *Depart for Capernaum headquarters arriving in mid-March (distance: 19 miles).*

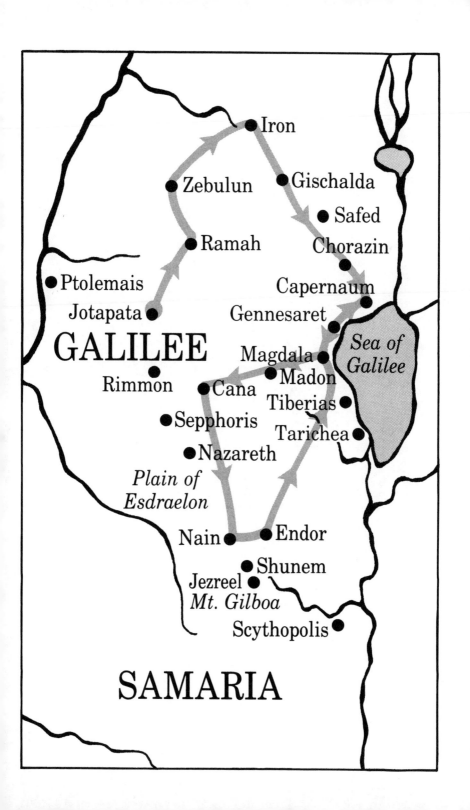

Towards the later part of January Jesus and the apostolic party continued north in their journey through Galilee.

In Ramah Jesus told his apostles that the son is naturally endowed with the life of the Father. (John 5:26) Here Jesus told them that he came forth from the Father, and many had received the Father's living spirit because they believed in him, but he declared to them that when he returned to the Father he would send his spirit into their hearts.

Said Jesus, *I will ask the Father, and he will give you another helper, that he may be with you forever; that is the spirit of truth, whom the world cannot receive, because it does not know him. But you know him because he abides with you and will forever.* (Luke 24:49, John 14:16-17)

And he went on to tell his followers that, *Every child of*

*God who follows the teaching of this spirit shall eventually know the will of God, and he who enters the kingdom has eternal life already and shall never perish.* (John 17:2-3)

All who heard these words of promise greatly cheered as the Jewish teaching had been confused and uncertain regarding the survival of the righteous. It must have been inspiring if not exhilarating to his followers to hear such a positive message of assurance about the eternal survival of all true believers.

Upon leaving Ramah, the apostolic party passed the small town of Zebulun, which was inhabited by a mixed race hardly Jew or Gentile, on their way to Iron.

They arrived in Iron the last week in January where Jesus and the apostles would teach and preach at the local synagogue. At this time all the synagogues of Galilee and Judah were open to him. (Matthew 4:23, Mark 1:39)

Iron was the site of extensive mineral mines and Jesus' fame as a healer had spread even to this remote town.

It was late afternoon on the third day at Iron that Jesus happened to encounter a leper on a narrow side street. As he drew near the squalid home, the leper made bold to accost him as he passed his door. This leper, although a believer in Jesus, felt he could not be received into the coming kingdom unless he could find a cure for his leprosy.

As a leper, he was forbidden among the Jews to attend the synagogue or otherwise engage in public worship, so in desperation he knelt before Jesus saying, *Lord, if only you would, you could make me clean. I have heard the message of your teachers, and I would enter the kingdom if I could be made clean.* (Matthew 8:1-3; Mark 1:40-42; Luke 5-12-13)

When Jesus saw this pathetic soul in all his affliction, his human heart and divine mind were moved with compassion. As he looked down upon him, he stretched forth his hand and, touching him, said, "I am willing; be cleansed." And immediately he was healed and his leprosy cleansed.

Now upon healing him, Jesus told this former leper not to tell a soul but to show himself to a priest and to offer those sacrifices commanded by Moses in testimony of his healing. (Matthew 8:4)

Instead of doing as Jesus had instructed, this man began to broadcast throughout the town that Jesus had cured his leprosy. (Mark 1:43-45; Luke 5:12-15)

Everyone in town knew this leper and when he was instantly healed, great throngs of the sick and afflicted set out to find Jesus. Beseeched by the multitudes, early the next morning Jesus and his followers left the village of Iron for Cana via Gischalda and Chorazin.

In Gischalda they spent two days, while tarrying a full week in Chorazin preaching the good news. Chorazin was a disappointment to Andrew and Abner and their associates as these people seemed little concerned and vaguely receptive to Jesus' gospel. (Luke 10:13)

Passing quietly through Capernaun they entered the village of Madon where they fared a little better. And so when Jesus announced, *Tomorrow we go to Cana,* (John 4:46) the apostles rejoiced. It was here, in the month of February two years earlier (AD 26), that Jesus turned water into wine at the wedding feast of Naomi and Johab, the son of Nathan.

On Tuesday, February 10, Jesus and his apostles arrived in Cana where they were met by Titus, a prominent citizen of Capernaun. (John 4:43)

Titus had a son who was critically ill and he beseeched Jesus to come over to Capernaun and heal his afflicted son who was at the point of death. (John 4:46-53)

While the apostles stood by in anticipation of another miracle, Jesus, looking upon the Father, said, *The power of God is in your midst, but except you see signs and behold wonders, you refuse to believe.* (John 4:48) Then Jesus bowed his head in a moment of silent meditation. Speaking to Titus he said, *Return to your home; your son will live.* (John 4:50)

Titus believed the word of Jesus and hastened home to Capernaum. Upon returning, his servants came out to greet him saying that his son was living and healing. Then Titus inquired of them at what hour the boy began to get better and they answered, *Yesterday about the seventh hour the fever left him.* (John 4:52-53) And this was the hour the father recalled Jesus had said, *Your son will live.* (John 4:53)

Now this was the second miracle to have occurred in Cana, attracting much attention to Jesus' ministry. Remembering the turning of water into wine and now the healing of a nobleman's son at so great a distance, the townspeople not only brought to him their sick and afflicted, but also sent messengers requesting that he heal sufferers at a distance.

Beseeched again by the multitudes, Jesus and his followers set out for the town of Nain.

By now the whole countryside was aroused by the numerous reports of Jesus' miraculous healings. Entering the city of Nain, Jesus and his followers came upon a great multitude of believers and many curious people following the pallbearers of a bier to the local cemetery.

As the funeral procession reached Jesus and his followers, a widow and her friends recognized the Master and besought him to bring her son back to life.

Surely he would not reject the pleas of such a distraught mother having lost her only child, they thought. Jesus was not to disappoint them. He stepped up to the coffin as the bearers came to a halt. Lifting the cover, Jesus looked upon the youth and said, *Young man I say unto you arise!* And the youth sat up and began to speak. (Luke 7:11-15)

To this wonder-seeking people a miracle was witnessed before their very eyes. The whole village of Nain was now aroused to the highest pitch of emotional frenzy. Fear seized many, some panicked, while still others fell to praying and glorifying God that a great prophet had risen among them. (Luke 7:16)

And so the word spread throughout Galilee and into Judea that Jesus had raised the widow's son from the dead. (Luke 7:17)

It was not Jesus' intention to go about working miracles for the wonderment of this sign-seeking generation, but when faced with such encounters, he never disappointed those genuine believers who only sought relief from their pain and suffering.

He admonished his apostles on a number of occasions to tell no one of these miraculous healings as was the case with the widow's son. They were true to their word; nevertheless, many a person witnessed this account and reported it years later to Luke, the physician, who duly recorded it in Scripture.

# Day 4:

# First Sabbath Encounter

*(March 30 to May 4, AD 28)*

# First Sabbath Encounter
## 5 Week Period
## March 30 — May 4, AD 28

**Tuesday, March 30:** *Jesus and Apostles leave Capernaum for Jerusalem. Camp south of Shunem (distance: 26 miles).*

**Wednesday, March 31:** *Apostolic party camps near base of Mount Sartaba (distance 26 miles).*

**Thursday, April 1:** *Camp outside Jericho (distance: 15 miles).*

**Friday, April 2:** *Set up headquarters at Bethany; home of Lazarus, long time friend of Jesus (distance: 12 miles).*

**Saturday, April 3:** *Jesus and Apostles enter Jerusalem (distance: 2 miles). Jesus, Peter, James and John invited to home of Simon, a wealthy Pharisee. Woman anoints the feet of Jesus. (Luke 7:37) Jesus relates to Simon the parable on forgiveness. (Luke 7:41-50)*

**Last week of April:** *Apostolic party leaves Jerusalem for Capernaum via Amathus (distance: 36 miles to Amathus).*

**Saturday, May 1:** *Confrontation with Jerusalem Pharisees outside Amathus over the plucking and eating of grain on the Sabbath. (Matt. 12:1-8, Mark 2:33-28, Luke 6:1-5) "I declare that the Sabbath was made for man, not man for the Sabbath." (Matt. 12:8)*

**Monday, May 3:** *Jesus and his Apostles arrive at Tarichea (distance: 32 miles). They take a boat to Bethsaida to escape Pharisees who journeyed with them (distance: 6 miles).*

**Tuesday, May 4:** *Depart for Capernaum. Jesus tells parable about putting new wine into old wine skins (distance: 2 miles). (Matt. 9:14-17, Mark 2:18-22, Luke 5:33-38)*

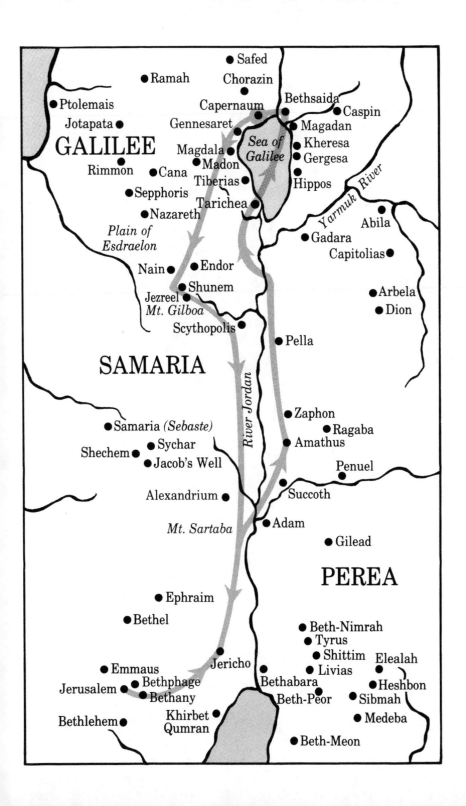

The first preaching tour culminated in a visit to the city of Endor, etched in posterity by the story of King Saul and the witch of Endor. (I Sam. 28:7-25) From here they returned to Capernaum, arriving at their Bethsaida headquarters in mid-March. They would tarry at Bethsaida, teaching along the seaside for a period of two weeks before heading south to Jerusalem and the Passover.

Jerusalem was a four-day trip going by way of the Jordan valley, and it was by far the most scenic route.

As the apostolic party headed south toward Samaria, they passed the ancient village of Shunem where the prophet Elisha had performed so many great works. The most beautiful maiden in all Israel was supposed to have lived there. Upon reaching the junction of Jezreel they headed east, recounting the many exploits of Ahab and Jezebel and of Jehu. Coming upon Mount

Gilboa they discussed the exploits of Saul who took his life on these slopes.

Rounding the base of Gilboa, they gazed upon the Greek city of Scythopolis and its splendid marble structures. From that junction they headed down into the tropical Jordan valley stopping to enjoy the exquisite beauty of this magnificent region. From their vantage point above the basin, they could observe the winding, glistening waters of the Jordan flowing towards the Dead Sea. As they gazed upon the valley, they admired the many luxurious fields of grain intermingled with flowering groves of pink blossomed oleanders. Beyond this lush valley paradise stood the majestic snow-capped Mount Herman to the north. It was truly a spectacular site to behold; a panorama of natural beauty. As they sat observing this scenic wonderment, each gave thanks to Yahweh for this gift of nature he bestowed upon his people.

On the second day's journey they passed the junction where the Jabbok intersects the Jordan, camping near the base of Mount Sartaba, the tallest mountain overlooking the Jordan. It was at the Alexandrian fortress occupying the summit of this mountain that Herod had imprisoned one of his wives and buried his two strangled sons.

By nightfall of the third day they had reached Jericho. The oasis at Jericho, the oldest inhabited city known to man, was famous for its date palms and for the sap of its balsam trees. This fragrant and medicinal "Balm of Gilead" was known for its curative affects on headaches and cataracts. Hot, sun-drenched Jericho was a winter haven for the wealthy, and to accommodate them, Herod had built three palaces there. An elaborate irrigation system, begun by the Hosmoneans and improved by Herod, brought water from springs as far as ten miles away. It was here, on the outskirts of town, the apostolic party would camp for the night.

Jesus and some of the apostles retired early, while the others sat around the campfire discussing Jericho's ancient past, recalling when in the days of Hiel, the Bethelite, *He laid the foundations thereof in Abiram, his first-born and set up its gates in his youngest son, Segub.* (I Kings 16:34)

They just couldn't understand how this petty king could sacrifice his only two sons, by burying them alive in the foundation holes of the city gates and "according to the word of the

Lord." What kind of God would allow such a thing to happen, let alone condone it? Did not Moses forbid such heathen practices?

In the months to come, Jesus would reveal to them the highest concept of God man could possibly envision, a God without enmity, a God of love and compassion.

From Jericho they soon began the climb of the hills leading to Jerusalem and to the eastern slopes of the Mount of Olives. It was there on these gentle slopes that lay the little village of Bethany, a small settlement at the edge of the Judean desert. Here Jesus and the apostles would spend the evening at the home of Lazarus.

Lazarus and his sisters, Martha and Mary, were long time friends and followers of Jesus. They were the children of a well-to-do and honorable Jew — one who had been the leading resident of this little village. Jesus always looked forward to his visits with these three whose parents had died some years earlier.

The apostles, tired from the day's journey, opted to bed down soon after their arrival. Jesus chose instead to spend this evening in conversation with his long-time friends. Little did the sisters know that in less than two years, their brother, Lazarus, would become a "cause celebre" by virtue of his death and resurrection.

The next morning they set out for Jerusalem, about two miles to the northwest.

Upon arriving in Jerusalem, an influential Pharisee named Simon invited Jesus and his personal associates, Peter, James and John to his home for a social meal. Simon knew Jesus, and was much impressed with his teachings.

Now it was customary in those days for the wealthy Pharisees to give alms to the poor and needy. On occasion they would announce their charitable deed with the blowing of a trumpet which they carried at their side as they bestowed their charity on some beggar. It was also the custom, when providing a banquet for distinguished guests, to leave the doors of the house open so that the street beggars could come in and stand along the walls behind the couches of the diners in order to receive a discarded morsel from time to time.

On this particular occasion, among those who came off the street was a woman of questionable moral repute, who had re-

55

cently become a believer in Jesus' gospel of the kingdom. This woman had a reputation as the former keeper of one of Jerusalem's high-class brothels located near the temple court of the gentiles. Although she had long since mended her ways, having accepted the teachings of Jesus, she was nevertheless compelled by the Pharisees to wear her hair down as a badge of harlotry.

Held in great disdain by the Pharisees, this woman nevertheless entered Simon's house and, standing behind Jesus as he reclined at meat, began to anoint his feet with a perfumed lotion she carried in an alabaster jar. (Luke 7:37)

As she ministered to the Master, her tears of gratitude wet his feet, which she proceeded to wipe with her hair. And when she finished this anointing, she continued weeping and kissing his feet.

All this time Simon was thinking to himself that if this man were a real prophet he would perceive that the woman anointing him held an unsavory reputation as a former brothel mistress. Surely a real prophet would not condone such actions from a notorious sinner.

But Jesus well knew the thoughts of Simon and spoke up saying, *Simon, I have something which I would like to say to you,* and Simon replied, *Say it teacher.* Then said Jesus: *A certain wealthy money-lender had two debtors. The one owed him 500 denarii and the other 50. When they were unable to repay, he graciously forgave them both. Which of them do you think, Simon, would love him the most?* And Simon answered, *I suppose the one whom he forgave more.* Then said Jesus, *You have rightly judged,* and pointing to the woman he continued to address Simon. *Do you see this woman? I entered your house as an invited guest, yet you gave me no water for my feet. This grateful woman has washed my feet with tears and wiped them with the hair of her head. You gave me no kiss of friendly greeting, but this woman, ever since she came in, has not ceased to kiss my feet. You neglected to anoint my head with oil, but she anointed my feet with precious lotions. And what is the meaning of all this? Simply that her many sins are forgiven, and this led her to love much. But those who have received but little forgiveness sometimes love but little.* And turning around towards the woman, he took her by the hand and lifting her up said, *You have indeed repented your sins, and they are forgiven. Your faith has saved you; go in peace.* (Luke 7:41-50)

When Simon and his friends heard these words of Jesus, they became alarmed and began to whisper among themselves, *Who is this man that he dares to forgive sins?* And when Jesus heard them murmuring, knowing what was in Simon's heart, said, I declare to all of you that the Father has opened the doors of the heavenly kingdom to all who have the faith to enter, and no man or association of men can close those doors even to the most humble soul or supposedly most flagrant sinner on earth if such sincerely seek an entrance. (Rev. 3:8) And Jesus, with Peter, James and John, took leave of their host to join their companions at camp in the garden of Gethsemane.

It was the last week in April when Jesus and the twelve departed from their Bethany headquarters near Jerusalem and began their journey back to Capernaum via Jericho and the Jordan.

About this time, the chief priest and the religious leaders of the Jews began to hold secret meetings to discuss Jesus and what to do with him in order to put an end to his teaching. Although they all agreed something must be done, they could not agree on a method.

They knew the civil authorities at Rome were not too alarmed by Jesus' preaching, therefore they must themselves set out to entrap him, then apprehend him on religious charges to be tried by the Sanhedrin. Accordingly, the day before Jesus' departure for Capernaum, a commission of six secret spies was appointed to follow Jesus to observe his actions and to record his words which might serve as blasphemy on which to indict him.

These six Jews caught up with the apostolic party, numbering about thirty at Jericho. They were able to join this group under the pretense of desiring to become disciples of Jesus.

They would remain with Jesus and his followers up to the time of the beginning of the second preaching tour in Galilee whereupon three of them would return to Jerusalem to report their findings to the chief priests and the Sanhedrin.

Crossing the Jordan the apostolic party headed for Capernaum via the town of Amathus, where they taught and preached and baptized for several days.

It was an early Sabbath morning that first day in May, when Jesus and his apostles presumed to leave Amathus for Capernaum. The six spies were hoping the apostolic party would set out this day as it was against Jewish law to so journey on the Sabbath. (Luke 6:7) But they were doomed to disappointment when Jesus instructed Andrew to proceed a distance of no more than a thousand yards, the legal Jewish Sabbath day's journey.

Their setback did not last long, however, for as the party passed along a narrow road, some of the apostles plucked ripened wheat grain and ate it. There was no thought of wrongdoing, as helping themselves to grain for their personal use was customary for travelers of that time. Nevertheless, these Pharisees seized upon this opportunity to confront Jesus when they saw Andrew rub the grain into his hand. At this point they approached Andrew saying, *Do you know that it is unlawful to pluck and rub grain on the Sabbath day?* Uncharacteristic of himself, Andrew snapped back saying, *But we are hungry and rub only sufficient for our needs, and since when did it become sinful to eat grain on the Sabbath day?* The Pharisees answered, *You do no wrong in eating but you do break the law in plucking and rubbing the grain between your hands; surely your master would not approve of such acts.* But Andrew was not in a mood to quibble over such minutia and told them that if it were not wrong to eat grain on the Sabbath, surely the rubbing of it between the hands was hardly more work than the chewing of the grain; so indignantly they approached Jesus who was walking with Matthew to protest his Sabbath breaking procedure. (Matthew 12:1-2, Mark 2:23-24, Luke 6:1-2)

Said these Pharisees, *Behold teacher, your apostles do that which is unlawful on the Sabbath day; they pluck, rub and eat grain. We are sure you will command them to cease.* Jesus responded, *You do well to remember the Sabbath to keep it holy, but, did you never read in Scripture that one day when David was hungry, he and they who were with him entered the house of God and ate the consecrated bread, which it was not lawful for anyone to eat save the priests? And did not David also give this bread to those who were with him?* (1 Sam. 21:3-6, Mark 2:23-27) *And have you not read in our law that it is lawful to do many needful things on the Sabbath day? My good men you do well to be zealous of the Sabbath, but you would do better to guard the health and well-being of your fellows. I declare to you that the Sabbath was made for man and not man for the Sabbath. And if you were present with us to watch my works, then I will openly proclaim that the Son of Man is lord even of the Sabbath.* (Matthew 12:8, Mark 2:28, Luke 6:5)

The Pharisees were astonished at these words of discernment and enraged at his presumption to be lord of the Sabbath. Nevertheless, for the remainder of that day, they kept to themselves and dared not to ask anymore questions.

Jesus' reaction to the Jewish traditions and rigid ceremonies was always positive, as he spent little time in negative denunciations. He taught that those who know God can enjoy the liberty of living without deceiving themselves by the licenses of sinning.

For a couple of days, Jesus and his apostles were able to avoid these spies bent on destroying his mission. It was Monday, around noon time, that Jesus and the twelve came to Bethsaida by boat from Tarichea, thus escaping those who journeyed with them for a day of rest. But by the next day, the spies and others had found them.

Early Tuesday evening, while Jesus was teaching, one of the six spies made bold to ask, *I was today talking with one of John's disciples who is here attending upon your teaching, and we were at a loss to understand why you never command your disciples to fast and pray as we Pharisees fast and as John bade his followers?* And Jesus answered him in the following manner: *Do the sons of the bride chamber fast while the bridegroom is with them? As long as the bridegroom remains with them, they can hardly fast. But the time is coming when the bridegroom shall be taken, and during those times, the children of the bride chamber undoubtedly will fast and pray. To pray is natural for the children of light, but fasting is not a part of the gospel of the kingdom of heaven. Be reminded that a wise tailor does not sew a piece of new and unshrunk cloth upon an old garment, lest when it is wet it shrink and produce a lesser rent. Neither do men put new wine into old wine skins, lest the new wine burst the skins so that both wine and skins perish. The wise man puts the new wine into fresh wine skins.* (Matthew 9:14-17, Mark 2:18-22, Luke 5:33-38)

Jesus also told his hearers that olden doctrines should not be replaced entirely by new ones, as that which is old and also true must abide. Likewise, that which is new, but false must be rejected. But that which is new and true, have the faith and

**59**

courage to accept. In essence, he was telling them to forsake not an old friend, for as new wine, so is a new friend; if it becomes old, you shall drink it with gladness. (Luke 5:39)

On May third, the apostolic party reached Bethsaida by boat from Terichea. For a period of five months — the dry season — Jesus and his apostles would remain camped at Bethsaida, along the northern shores of the Sea of Galilee. From their seaside camp they would teach the gospel of the kingdom to new evangelists while training them to become ministers among men.

There was no standardized or dogmatic formulation of theologic doctrines; to the contrary, the Master denounced such slavish devotion to meaningless ceremonials.

These student-evangelists readily took to the gospel teachings because they so whole-heartedly believed in the Master himself. In Jesus, they could see no sign of social prejudice, racial intolerance, or religious superstition. He was totally unpretentious in his teachings of substituting clean hearts for clean hands as the mark of true religion. His demeanor appealed to the common man, unsophisticated and devoid of all pretensions of vanity and hypocrisy.

He dared to proclaim man's spiritual freedom and taught that all men are in truth sons of the living God. Both the man and his message were transforming; and because of this, multitudes would follow him for weeks just to hear his gracious words and behold his simple life.

During this period, from May to October, there were many converts to Jesus' gospel, in spite of the fact few miracles were performed. Two notable encounters did take place, however, both towards the end of this interlude of teaching and training.

The first encounter occurred on the second Sabbath before the apostles second preaching tour of Galilee. Jesus had just finished speaking at the Capernaum synagogue when a man with a withered hand, induced by the Pharisees, approached him saying, *Is it lawful to be healed on the Sabbath or should I seek help on another day?* (Matthew 12:10, Luke 14:3)

The scribes and the Pharisees were watching him closely to see if Jesus healed on the Sabbath, in order that they might find reason to accuse him. When Jesus saw the man and heard his words, he perceived that he had been sent by the Pharisees. Addressing them, the Master said, *What man shall there be among you, who shall have a sheep, and if it falls into a pit on the Sabbath, will not take hold of it and lift it out? I ask you, is it lawful on the Sabbath to do good or to do evil, to save a life or to destroy it?* Jesus well knew this man was sent to tempt him to show mercy on the Sabbath, but all present, by their silence, had condoned an act of kindness of lifting an unfortunate sheep out of a pit, even on the Sabbath. And Jesus said to them, *I proclaim it is lawful to do good to men on the Sabbath for how much more valuable is a man than a sheep!*

As they all stood before the Master in silence, Jesus, addressing the man with the withered hand, said *If you have the faith to be healed, I bid you stretch out your hand.* And as the man stretched forth his hand, it was made whole. (Matthew 12:9-14, Mark 3:1-6, Luke 6:6-11)

Although many marveled at this act of healing, the Pharisees became angered; and notwithstanding it was the Sabbath, hastened to Tiberias to take council with Herod attempting to secure the Herodians as allies against Jesus. But Herod, at this time, refused to take action against Jesus, advising these delegates to take their complaints to Jerusalem. (Matthew 12:14)

The second miracle of faith-healing occurred some two weeks later. It was Friday afternoon, the first day of October and Jesus was holding the last of his discussions with his apostles, evangelists and other leaders of his soon to be disbanded camp. Knowing this was to be his last session with these disciples before their next preaching tour, the enlarged living room of the Zebedee home was packed to the gills by followers straining their ears to catch some part of Jesus' discourse. Seated among his followers were the six Pharisees from Jerusalem who occupied seats in the front row. They, along with Jesus' friends, were about to witness one of the most unique episodes in Jesus' public ministry.

As Jesus was about to speak, standing in the middle of the Zebedee living room, he was interrupted by a commotion directly above him. A man was being lowered from the roof of the building on a couch which now sat just before him. Apparently this man, a paralytic, had heard of Jesus' powers to heal by a neighbor friend, Aaron the stone mason, who had recently been healed of a withered hand only a few weeks before.

Summoning his friends, he had them carry him to the Zebedee home on a small couch. His comrades tried to gain entrance but too many people surrounded both the front and back doors. Undaunted by his failure to gain entrance, the paralytic directed his friends to procure ladders in hopes of gaining entrance through the roof. His perseverance rewarded him, as he was able to be lowered by ropes through the roof to the very feet of the Master.

Everyone marveled at the sick man's enterprise and the dedication of his friends. And, seeing their faith, Jesus said to the paralytic, *My son, fear not, your sins are forgiven.* (Matthew 9:2, Mark 2:5, Luke 5:20)

When the Pharisees from Jerusalem and their associates, the scribes and lawyers who sat with them, heard this pronouncement by Jesus, they said to themselves: *Why does this man speak this way? Does he not understand such words are blasphemy? Who can forgive sin but God?* (Matthew 9:3, Mark 2:7, Luke 5:21)

Jesus, perceiving in his spirit that they were reasoning that way within their own minds among themselves, spoke to them saying, *Why do you reason so within your own hearts? Who are you that you sit in judgment over me? What is the difference whether I say to this paralytic, 'your sins are forgiven, or arise, take your bed and walk?' But in order that you may know that the Son of Man has authority on earth to forgive sins, I will say to this afflicted man, 'arise, take up your bed and go home.'* (Matthew 9:4-6, Mark 2:7-11)

And when Jesus had thus spoken, the paralytic arose and, as the room parted, he walked out before them all. All who witnessed this event were amazed and astonished; and many prayed and glorified God, confessing that they had never seen anything like this. (Matthew 9:2-8, Mark 2:1-12, Luke 5:17-26)

After this remarkable episode at the Zebedee home, the fame of Jesus had spread to all parts of Palestine and through all of Syria and the surrounding countries.

*Day 5:*

# **T**he Capernaum Crisis

*(Mid-March to April 30, AD 29)*

# The Capernaum Crisis
## 6 Week Period
## Mid-March to April 30 AD 29

**Monday, March 21:** *Jesus heals Legion, the lunatic, at Kheresa on the eastern shores of the Sea of Galilee. (Matt. 8:28-32, Mark 5:2-13, Luke 8:26-37) Apostolic party sails for Capernaum (distance: 6 miles).*

**Tuesday, March 22:** *Jesus heals woman of scourging hemorrhage. (Matt. 9:20-22, Mark 5:30-34, Luke 8:43-48)*

**Sunday, March 27:** *Jesus and Apostles sail for park south of Bethsaida-Julias (distance 4 miles).*

**Wednesday, March 30:** *Jesus feeds the 5,000 at the park south of Bethsaida-Julias, on eastern shores of Lake Capernaum. (Matt. 14:17-21, Mark 6:38-44, Luke 9:13-17, John 6:5-13)*

**Thursday, March 31:** *Jesus and the twelve cross over to Genesaret for several days of rest (distance: 5 miles).*

**Sunday, April 3:** *Apostolic party departs Bethsaida for Jerusalem via Gerasa and Philadelphia (distance to Philadelphia: 65 miles).*

**Wednesday, April 6:** *Arrive in Bethany late evening (distance: 36 miles). Spend time with Lazarus, Martha and Mary.*

**Sunday, April 24:** *Jesus and Apostles leave Jerusalem for Bethsaida, stopping off in coastal cities of Joppa, Caesarea and Ptolemais (distance: 90 miles to Ptolemais).*

**Friday, April 29:** *Arrive late Friday evening in Bethsaida from Ptolemais (distance: 30 miles).*

**Saturday, April 30:** *Jesus speaks at Capernaum Synagogue (distance: 2 miles). I am the bread of life. (John 6:35) He who believes has eternal life. (John 6:47) Jesus heals distraught youth who is blind, dumb and possessed of evil spirits. (Matt. 12:22, Luke 11:14) In my Father's Kingdom the tree is known by its fruit. (Matt. 12:33)*

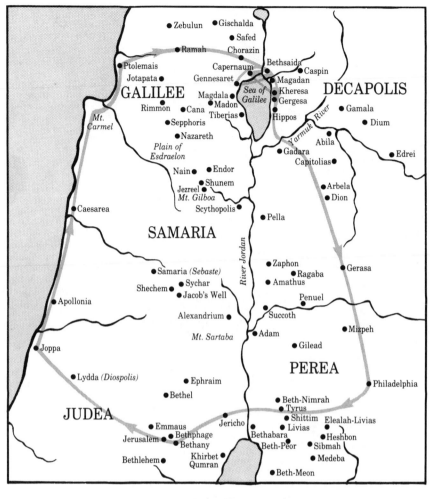

**Detail:**

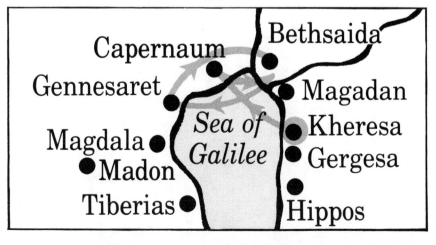

**L**ess than two months before Jesus was to speak in the Capernaum synagogue, there occurred several events that would arouse the curiosity and fears of both the religious leaders and the civil rulers throughout Galilee and Judea.

The first such event occurred along the eastern shores of the Sea of Galilee when Jesus, his disciples, and a group of about 40 followers landed near the small town of Kheresa.

It was early evening when they landed, and since the water was calm and the night was clear, Jesus and his followers all chose to remain on their boats until morning.

Although it was near the end of the rainy season, the waters were unusually low for this time of year, being about 700 feet below sea level. As they arose, about sunrise, they could see along the entire hillside a score of caverns that had been hewn out of rock for the purpose of housing many an ancient sepulchre. About halfway up the hillside, in a level area, lay the little cemetery of Kheresa.

Inhabiting the tombs and abandoned sepulchers was a demented lunatic named Legion. From time to time he would experience terrible spells of maniacal insanity and would terrorize all who chanced to meet him, flailing his arms with chains from previous incarcerations still attached, moaning the sounds of the half crazed lunatic he was.

As Jesus and his party passed by this man crouching like an animal, Legion threw himself upon the feet of Jesus, beseeching him to cast the demons out of him.

We are told by Matthew, Mark, and Luke that this man was made whole and that the demons residing in him were transferred to a herd of swine where they rushed headlong over a precipice to their destruction in the sea below. This story of the Kheresa lunatic and the swine spread rapidly among the villagers and neighboring communities and was the first of several miraculous encounters that would ferment fear and apprehension among the Pharisees at Jerusalem. (Matthew 8:28-32, Mark 5:2-13, Luke 8:26-37)

By the time Jesus and his disciples reached Capernaum, great crowds were waiting to see what further miracles might unfold, of which they might bear eye witness. Some of the throng were new observers from the Jerusalem Sanhedrin, who were now looking for an excuse to arrest and convict the Master.

As Jesus and his party entered town, they were greeted by Jairus, the ruler of the local synagogue. The Master had been told of Jairus' daughter's illness to the point of death and was asked to heal her. Jesus agreed and, as they headed for home, he perceived someone having reached out to touch his garment. When Jesus asked who touched him, his eyes fell upon a woman who had been afflicted with a scourging hemorrhage. When this woman, Veronica of Caesarea-Philippi, realized she had been immediately healed, she fell at his feet. And Jesus said to her, *Daughter, your faith has made you well. Go in peace.* (Matthew 9:20-22, Mark 5:30-34, Luke 8:43-48)

As Jesus, Peter, James, and John approached the home of Jairus, a servant came out saying, *Trouble not Master, your daughter is dead.* But Jesus said to Jairus, *Fear not, only believe.* (Mark 5:35) When he entered the house, mourners were abound weeping and wailing, along with flute players, all contributing to a tumultuous commotion.

When he told the mourners that the child had not died, but was in fact asleep, they laughed him to scorn. Putting them out of the room, Jesus approached the young girl and told her to rise. Immediately she awakened from her coma and began to talk, whereupon Jesus directed the mother and father to give her something to eat. (Matthew 9:18-25, Mark 5:22-43, Luke 8:41-55)

As the news of these miracles began to spead, everywhere Jesus went the sick and afflicted were waiting for him. Jesus well knew that for some it meant healing — an immediate cure for their affliction. To others, it meant the chance to witness the wonder-working of the supernatural, and to others still, an alarming threat to their existence. It was this latter group of spiritually blinded, tradition bent Jewish religious leaders that had vowed to destroy the Son of Man. They would see to it that if he broke the laws of Moses, he would suffer the consequences.

Meanwhile, as his popularity increased through a number of recent miracles, Jesus found it increasingly difficult to shed the enormous throngs that had taken up following him, seeking to witness more miracles. It was for this reason that he decided on Friday, March 25, to declare a furlough of one week that his followers might go home to their friends for a few days before heading to Jerusalem for the Passover. By Sunday, more than half of his disciples refused to leave him and the multitude was increasing daily. David Zebedee, the older brother of James and John, desired to establish a new encampment, but Jesus refused.

Instead, he would plan a small retreat for just himself and his twelve apostles on the eastern shores of Lake Capernaum. It was this same day that Jesus and the twelve apostles sneaked out of camp in a small boat and headed for the beautiful park south of Bethsaida — Julias, on the opposite shore. (John 6:17-24) But the people were not to be denied, and when they spotted the boat and the direction it was headed, they hired every boat available and took out in pursuit. (Mark 6:45)

What started to be a quiet retreat ended that afternoon with a gathering of more than a thousand people. By Monday, more than 3,000 had gathered, and by Wednesday, some 5,000 people were at the park south of Bethsaida — Julias.

Since Jesus and the twelve had not anticipated this large a

gathering, the question of how to feed them was paramount. Philip had provided food for three days and they were well into their third day. So when Jesus asked of their chore boy, John Mark, the lad informed Andrew that there were only five barley loaves and two dried fish, and Peter was quick to add, *We have yet to eat this evening.* (Matthew 14:17-21, Mark 6:38-44, Luke 9:12-13, John 9:13-17)

Then Jesus asked that the basket be brought to him. Directing the people to sit in groups of 100, Jesus, after giving thanks, broke the bread and fish and gave it to his apostles to pass out to some fifty groups. And when the multitude had eaten and were filled, Jesus asked that they gather up the broken pieces that remained so that nothing would be lost. When the fragments were gathered, they had twelve baskets full. (Matthew 14:17-21, Mark 6:38-44, Luke 9:13-17, John 6:5-13)

Having thus satisfied their hunger, there was but one unanimous reaction among the multitude, and that was to crown Jesus king. After all, they thought, were we not fed to satiation and should not the power to feed carry with it the power to rule?

But this was not to be, he told them, and announced to them that he and his apostles would withdraw for a few days of rest before going up to Jerusalem for the Passover. (John 6:15)

The news of the feeding of the five thousand and the attempt to make Jesus king had spread throughout all Galilee and Judea, and although it aroused widespread curiosity among the people, it also aroused the suspicions and fears of the religious leaders and civil rulers in this region. From this time on, they would vehemently plot his destruction.

The apostolic party rested at Gennesaret and for the twelve, it was a time of deep soul searching. (Matthew 14:34, Mark 6:53)

Jesus' declining this honor of being crowned king was a disappointment to many of his followers, as they genuinely felt he was the promised Messiah. For a long time these Jews had been taught that the Messiah would return the land and its people to their past glory — that the promised land would once again flow with milk and honey, and that the bread of life would be bestowed upon them as manna from heaven was supposed to have fallen upon their forefathers in the wilderness.

Gennesaret was a sobering sojourn for the twelve , as they listened to their Lord regarding the trials ahead.

The mood of the apostles seemed to rise with the exhilaration of the multitudes. Just a few days before, the anticipation of Jesus receiving the Crown of David had the populace astir with excitement. Many of these people were miracle-seekers and material-minded, half-hearted believers who could not fathom Jesus' proclamation of a spiritual kingdom in the hearts of men. They were seeking a Messiah-king who would return the Jewish nation to the military prominence it once enjoyed under David. When Jesus refused to accept this role, many turned away. In less than one month's time, his enthusiastic followers, who numbered over 50,000 in Galilee alone, shrank to less than 500.

By the second day of their sojourn at Gennesaret, the apostles were downcast and dejected, as they were told by the Master what could be expected of the Jerusalem religious rulers as they conspired with Herod Antipas to affect their destruction.

Jesus did his best to soften his apostles' disillusionment by telling them his mission was not to sit on David's throne, and that his teaching of spiritual truths was not to be advanced by material wonders.

The purpose of his feeding the 5,000 was not to perform a wonder-working supernatural miracle, but to offer bodily sustenance to those genuine believers who gathered to hear his message of another kingdom — the Kingdom of Heaven. (John 6:26)

On Sunday, April 3, the apostles started out on their journey from Bethsaida to Jerusalem. It was a circuitous route by way of Gerasa and Philadelphia to avoid the multitudes.

Late Wednesday, the apostolic party arrived at Bethany where Jesus and the apostles spent the night, hearing from Lazarus and others about the resentment building against them in Jerusalem.

The Passover was uneventful in terms of Jesus preaching, as he only entered Jerusalem once, on the day of the feast. On Sunday, April 24, the apostolic party departed for Bethsaida, going by way of the coast cities of Joppa, Caesarea, and Ptolemais. From there they headed inland, by way of Ramah and Chorazin to Bethsaida, where they arrived on Friday evening. (Matthew 16:13)

The next morning, Saturday, April 30, Jesus was to speak in the new synagogue, and he well knew it would be the last time he would be permitted to speak there.

Jairus, the leader of the Capernaum synagogue, was beseeched by the Jerusalem leaders not to let Jesus speak. As a man of honor, he told them that it was already arranged, and he would not change his mind.

Accordingly, Jesus came to the synagogue knowing full well the Jewish leaders were busily stacking the congregation with those sympathetic to their cause. The day before, some fifty Pharisees and Sadducees had arrived from Jerusalem, along with some thirty of the leaders and rulers of the neighboring synagogues. These Jewish religious leaders were acting under the direct orders of the Jerusalem Sanhedrin to establish open warfare on Jesus and his disciples. They had come to embarrass and to entrap the Master with questions, the answers to which might indict him with the high Jewish court, the Sanhedrin. Occupying the seats of honor alongside these Jewish leaders were the official observers of Herod Antipas, there to find cause why the populace attempted to make Jesus king of the Jews in the domain of his brother, Philip.

An air of hostility pervaded this congregation and Jesus very well knew why. At the feeding of the 5,000 he had challenged their ideas of a material Messiah, and now he was about to attack their concept of the Jewish deliverer. He was about to tell them he had come to proclaim spiritual liberty, teach eternal truth and foster living faith, not for purposes of establishing a temporary material kingdom as the heir to the throne of David.

The sermon Jesus was about to deliver would require a decision from each and every individual gathered in the synagogue, to choose God's way or man's way. It was designed to appeal to the truly religious brotherhood of mankind, not to the proud, arrogant, and self-righteous.

Jesus' sermon was introduced by a reading from the law as found in Deuteronomy. *But it shall come to pass, if this people will not hearken to the voice of God, that the curses of transgression shall surely overtake them,* . . . (Deuteronomy 28:15). And when this reading was over, Jesus began to read from Jeremiah, whose situation with the priest and rulers he found somewhat analogous to his own. *'If you will not hearken to the words of my servants, the prophets whom I have sent you, then will I make this house like Shiloh, and I will make this city a curse to all the nations of the earth.'* . . . *'The Lord sent me to prophesy against this house and against this city all the words which you have heard. Now therefore amend your ways and reform your doings and obey the voice of the Lord your God that you may escape the evil which has been pronounced against you.' When the princes of Judah heard these things, they sat in judgment of Jeremiah, saying: 'This man is worthy to die for he has prophesied against our city and you have heard him with your own ears.'*(Jeremiah 26:4-11)

Although the priest and teachers of that day sought to kill Jeremiah, the judges were content in placing him up to his elbows in the mirey pit of a dungeon. That is what this people did to the Prophet Jeremiah when he obeyed the Lord's command to warn his brethren of their impending political downfall. And Jesus asked the religious leaders and chief priest what they intended to do with the man who dares to warn them of the day of their spiritual doom. Would they also put to death the teacher who dares to proclaim the word of the Lord, and who fears not to point out the way of light which leads to the entrance to the Kingdom of Heaven?

As Jesus looked upon the assembled Pharisees and Sadducees, he admonished them for seeking not for truth and righteousness in which to better serve their fellow man, but for the bread and goods of life, in which they had not labored. They were looking not to fill their souls with the word of life but only to fill their bellies with the bread of ease.

Glancing about his audience, he said: *My brethren, labor not for the meat which perishes, but rather seek for the spiritual food that nourishes even to eternal life; and this is the bread of life which the Son gives to all who will take it and eat, for the Father has given the Son his life without measure. And when you asked me, 'What must we do to perform the works of God?' I plainly told you, 'This is the work of God, that you believe him whom he has sent.'* (John 6:27-29)

And then, pointing up to the device of a pot of manna decorating the lintel of the new synagogue embellished as it was with grape clusters, Jesus said: *You have thought your forefathers in the wilderness ate manna — the bread of heaven — but I say to you that Moses did not give you the true bread of life. The bread of heaven is that which comes down from God and gives eternal life to the men of the world.* (John 6:31-33)

*And when you say to me, 'Give us this living bread,' I will answer: I am this bread of life. He who comes to me shall not hun-*

ger *while he who believes me shall never thirst. You have seen me, lived with me, and beheld my works, yet you believe not that I come forth from the Father. But to those who do believe — fear not. All those led of the Father shall come to me, and he who comes to me shall in no way be cast out.*

*And now I declare to you, once and for all time, that I have come down upon earth, not to do my own will, but the will of Him who sent me. And this is the will of Him who sent me: that everyone who beholds the Son and who believes him shall have eternal life.* (John 6:35-40)

Now there were a number of priests who, upon hearing this declaration of sonship with the Father, became incensed and one of them made bold to ask, *But are you not Jesus of Nazareth, the son of Joseph, the carpenter? Are not your father and mother well-known to many of us? How then is it that you appear here in God's house and declare that you have come down from heaven?* (John 6:42, Luke 4:22)

By now there was much murmuring in the synagogue and the fury was about to unleash when Jesus stood up and said, *Let us be patient; the truth never suffers from honest examination. I am all that you say and more. The Father and I are one; the Son does that which the Father teaches him while all those who are given to the Son by the Father, the Son will receive to himself. You have read where it is written by the Prophets, 'You shall all be taught by God,' and that, 'Those whom the Father teaches will also hear his Son.'* (Isaiah 54:13) *Everyone who yields to the Father's indwelling spirit will eventually come to me. Not that anyone has seen the Father, except the one who is from God; he has seen the Father.* (John 6:41-46)

*Verily, verily I say to you, the Son who has come down from heaven has surely seen the Father and those who truly believe this Son already have eternal life.* (John 6:33, 47)

*I am this bread of life. Your fathers ate manna in the wilderness and are dead. But this bread which comes down from God, if a man eats thereof, he shall never die in spirit. I repeat, I am this living bread, and every soul who attains the realization of this united nature of God and man shall live forever. And this bread of life which I give to all who will receive is my own flesh and blood.* (John 6:48-51)

When Jesus finished speaking, the ruler of the synagogue dismissed the congregation, but they would not leave. Murmuring amongst themselves, they stayed some three hours to discuss with Jesus what he meant by his unabashed pronouncements. (John 6:41)

One of the visiting Pharisees shouted, what did he mean by telling them he was the bread of life? *How can you give us your flesh to eat?* (John 6:52)

And Jesus answered: *You cannot eat my flesh nor can you drink my blood, but you can become one in spirit with me as I am one in spirit with the Father. You can be nourished by the eternal word of God, which is indeed the bread of life, and which has been bestowed in the likeness of mortal flesh; and you can be watered in soul by the divine spirit, which is truly the water of life. The Father has sent me into the world to show how he desires to indwell and direct all men; and I have so lived this life in the flesh as to inspire all men likewise ever to seek to know and do the will of the indwelling heavenly Father.* (John 6:53-65)

At this point, one of the Jerusalem leaders who had come to agitate and find fault with Jesus, hoping to entrap him, made bold to ask: *We noticed that neither you nor your apostles wash your hands properly before you eat bread. You must well know that you are transgressing the traditions of the elders. Why is it that you show such disrespect for the laws of our elders?* (Matthew 15:1-2, Mark 7:5)

Jesus well knew this man was set on entrapping him for flouting the sacred laws of the Jews, as he was a Pharisaic commissioner of the Jerusalem Sanhedrin. No matter how scarce water might be, these traditionally enslaved Jews would never think of dispensing with the required ceremonial washing of hands before every meal. It was their belief that, "It is better to die than to transgress the commandments of the elders." And so this question was asked because it was reported that Jesus had once said, "Salvation is a matter of clean hearts rather than clean hands."

And when Jesus heard the Pharisee speak, he answered him thusly, *Rightly did Isaiah prophesy of you hypocrites, as it is written:*

> *'this people honors me with their lips,*
> *but their heart is far from me*
> *but in vain, do they worship me*
> *teaching as their doctrines the precepts of men.'* (Isaiah 29:13)

**75**

*You persist in neglecting the commandment of God, while you hold to the tradition of men. Altogether willing are you to reject the word of God while you maintain your own traditions. And in many other ways, do you dare to set up your own teachings above the law and the prophets.* (Matthew 15:3, Mark 7:6-9)

*But hear and understand all of you. It is not that which enters the mouth that spiritually defiles the man but rather that which proceeds out of the mouth and from the heart.* (Matthew 15:15)

Some of the people did not fully grasp the meaning of Jesus' words and in an attempt to mollify the crowd, knowing full well the proud Pharisees were offended, Simon Peter asked of Jesus: *Lest some of your hearers be unnecessarily offended would you explain to us the meaning of these words?* And Jesus said to Peter, *Are you also hard of understanding? Know you that every plant my heavenly Father has not planted shall be rooted up. You cannot compel men to love the truth. Many of these teachers are blind guides. And you know that if the blind lead the blind, both shall fall into the pit. I declare it is not that which enters the body by the mouth or gains access to the mind through the eyes and ears, that defiles the man. Man is only defiled by that evil which may originate within the heart, and which finds expression in the words and deeds of such unholy persons. Do you not know it is from the heart that there come forth evil thoughts of murder, theft, adultery, fornication, together with jealousy, pride, anger, revenge and false witness? And these are the things that defile the man, and not that they eat bread with ceremonially unclean hands.* (Matthew 15:12-20)

The Master had exposed the folly of the whole rabbinic system of the rules and regulations which was represented by the oral law — the tradition of the elders — and these Pharisees would not forget it. To them, eating with unwashed hands was tantamount to sleeping with a harlot, and both were punishable by excommunication.

Many of the congregation understood the words of Jesus and were heartened by them, while others stood confused. And still others, the Jerusalem contingent, resentfully and secretly plotted against him. (John 7:31-32)

In the midst of their discussions, one of the Pharisees from Jerusalem brought to Jesus a distraught youth, blind and dumb, and possessed of evil spirits.

When Jesus saw this pathetic lad, he was so moved with compassion he beckoned the boy to him and immediately made him whole by casting out the evil spirit. (Matthew 12:22, Luke 11:14)

When the Pharisees saw that the lad could speak and see, their hatred of Jesus intensified and they accused him of casting out demons by Beelzebub, the prince of devils. Said one Pharisee, *Have nothing to do with this man, he is in partnership with Satan.* (Matthew 12:24, Mark 3:22, Luke 11:14)

And knowing their thoughts, Jesus said to them, *Any kingdom divided against itself cannot stand, and if a house be divided against itself, it shall not stand. How can Satan cast out Satan? If Satan cast out Satan, he is divided against himself; how then shall his kingdom stand?* (Matthew 12:24-26, Mark 3:22-26, Luke 11:14-18)

*But you should know that no one can enter into the house of a strong man and carry off his property except to first overpower and bind that strong man. And then he will plunder his house. And so, if I, by the power of Beelzebub, cast out demons, by whom do your sons cast them out? Consequently, they shall be your judges. But if I, by the spirit of God, cast out demons, then has the kingdom of God truly come upon you.* (Matthew 12:27-29, Mark 3:27, Luke 11:20-22)

*If these Pharisees were not blinded by prejudice and misled by fear and pride, they could easily have perceived that one who is greater than devils stood in their midst.* Said the Master, *You compel me to declare that he who is not with me is against me, while he who gathers not with me scatters abroad.* (Matthew 12:30-31) *To those of you who harbor premeditated malice, and knowingly ascribe the works of God to the doings of the devil, verily, verily, I say to you and your sins shall be forgiven, even all your blasphemies, but whosoever shall blaspheme against God with deliberation and wicked intention shall never obtain forgiveness. And those persistent workers of iniquity will never seek nor receive forgiveness. They are guilty of the sin of eternally rejecting divine goodness.* (Matthew 12:31-32, Mark 3:28-29, Luke 12:10)

As Jesus stood before a number of the Jerusalem Pharisees, he told them that they had a choice between doing the will of the Father or following their self-chosen ways of darkness. Said Jesus, *As you now choose, so shall you eventually be. You must either make the tree good and its fruit good, or else will the tree become corrupt and its fruit corrupt; for in my Father's kingdom the tree is known by its fruits.* (Matthew 12:33)

And then as the Son of God standing before men, Jesus looked upon them and said, *But some of you who are vipers, how can you, having already chosen evil, bring forth good fruits? For the mouth speaks out of that which fills the heart.* (Matthew 12:24, Luke 6:45)

And he went on to say, *The good man out of his good treasure brings forth what is good; and the evil man out of his evil treasure, brings forth what is evil. And I say to you that every careless word that men shall speak, they shall render account for in the day of judgment. For by your words, you shall be justified and by your words, you shall be condemned.* (Matthew 12:35-37)

Now these Pharisees were learned men, and recognized as such by the people. They bowed to God, but stooped to no man. They were proud and self-righteous; but somehow the intimidating presence of the man of Galilee threatened their very existence. They were not about to relinquish their control over the people, especially to a Galilean.

Pondering the Master's words, one of these Pharisees made bold to ask, *Teacher, we would have you give us a predetermined sign which we will agree upon as establishing your authority and right to teach.* And when Jesus heard this, he exclaimed, *This faithless and adulterous generation seeks a token, but no sign shall be given you than that which you already have, and that which you shall see when the Son of Man departs from among you.* (Matthew 12:38, 6:4; Mark 8:11; Luke 11:16)

When Jesus had finished speaking, he beckoned his apostles to depart from the synagogue and they journeyed silently back to Bethsaida.

This was one of the most significant episodes in Jesus' early career, as this admonishment to the Jewish leaders did much to separate the genuine truth seekers from the faithless miracle seekers.

Failing to grasp Jesus' real mission on earth, many of his associates deserted the cause that Sabbath day in April, AD 29. (John 6:66)

The great significance of the crisis at Capernaum was that man had to make a choice of following his intellectual inclinations or his spiritual leadings — a religion of the mind versus a religion of the spirit. The spiritual religion of Jesus meant effort, struggle, faith, love, loyalty and progress. The intellectual religion of the Pharisees was a theology of authority, enslaving them to the traditions of the past.

A religion of tradition was a safe harbor for these pious Pharisees. The religion of Jesus was capable of withstanding the high seas of adversity but required humility, the subordination of man's will to God's will. Faith was its cornerstone.

The Capernaum episode, for some, represented a victory for their misguided egos. Misguided in the sense that they allowed their egos to be superimposed upon conscience, rather than subdued by conscience, creating an egocentric personality fed by the pride of self-adulation. They had confused self-admiration with self-respect. One inhibits spiritual growth, the other enhances it.

Self-respect is always coordinate with the love and service of one's fellows, and it is not possible to respect oneself more than that person can love his neighbors; the one is the measure of the capacity of the other.

The measure of spiritual growth in man is his faith in God and his love for his fellow man.

To be sure, these Pharisees were beneath God, but they had elevated themselves above their fellow man. They knew God as their Father, but they could not accept their fellow man as their brother. More often than not, they drew attention to their deeds, always displaying their righteous cloak of respectability. Their pride was their barrier to spiritual growth.

Living faith does not foster bigotry, persecution or intolerance, but to these spiritually blind Jewish leaders, their authority to teach was being threatened by this provincial Galilean. The high court of the Sanhedrin would take whatever course was necessary to remove this threat. On this very evening, Saturday, Apirl 30, special commissioners, representing the Jerusalem Sanhedrin, were meeting with Herod Antipas to plot the Master's overthrow.

Chuza, one of Herod's advisors, had heard Jesus decline the throne of David and correctly reported that Jesus had not intended to meddle in earthly affairs, but instead called for the establishment of a spiritual brotherhood which he called the kingdom of heaven. Herod relied upon this information and refused to take action against Jesus, distrusting the motives of these men. It was a mutual distrust, as Herod was considered an outsider, an Idumean, not a Jew. He had inherited the rule of his father who had ingratiated himself with Rome in the year 40 BC and by acclamation of the Senate was given the power to rule not only Idumea but all of Palestine as its king under Roman authority.

Although Herod Antipas, much like his father, adopted a gingerly tolerance toward Judea's more zealous religious groups he was always subject to their scrutiny as a foreigner, an upstart Idumean of questionable lineage, no matter his nominal religion.

These hostile Sanhedrin leaders knew their Scripture well, especially the passage that read: *One from among your brethren you shall set as king over you; you may not put a foreigner over you.* (Deut. 17:15)

From years of foreign rule, Egyptian, Assyrian, Babylonian, Persian, Greek and Roman, the Jewish mind became increasingly distrustful of foreign domination and Herod, as a puppet of Rome was no exception.

Unyielding to their demands, Herod could find no fault in Jesus, regarding him no more than a harmless religious fanatic, but the Sanhedrin representatives were not to be denied. Within one week of the Capernaum episode they would take official action to close all synagogues in Palestine to him. On Friday, at the instigation of the Jerusalem Pharisees, in an unprecedented move, the Capernaum synagogue was closed to his teachings and immediately Jairus, its chief ruler, resigned and opening aligned himself with Jesus.

The closing of the synagogues represented the first official act by the Jewish leaders to discredit Jesus' popularity with the people.

Jesus had violated no rules, did not preach against the laws of the elders, nor did he attempt to subvert these congregations. His only crime was that by teaching truth, he became a threat to established authority.

This was not only unacceptable, it was intolerable and within one week of the Capernaum crisis, the question yet to be answered by these Jerusalem Pharisees was, "What shall we do with Jesus?"

*Day 6:*

# **T**he Phoenician Journey

*(June 9 to July 23, AD 29)*

# The Phoenician Journey
### 6 Week Period
### June 9 — August 4, AD 29

**Thursday, June 9:** *Casearea Philippi to Sidon via Luz (distance: 28 miles). Sidon — Jesus heals woman's daughter. (Matt. 15:21-28)*

**Sunday, July 10:** *Sidon to Tyre via Sarepta (distance: 22 miles). Tyre — Jesus teaches that a "wise man builds his foundation well (upon a rock) for growth of noble character." (Matt. 7:24-27, Luke 6:47-49)*

**Sunday, July 24:** *Apostolic party heads home.*

**Tuesday, July 26:** *Ptolemais (distance: 26 miles).*

**Thursday, July 28:** *Jotapata (distance: 11 miles).*

**Sunday, July 31:** *Ramah (distance: 10 miles).*

**Monday, August 1:** *Zebulun (distance: 5 miles).*

**Wednesday, August 3:** *Gischalda to Chorazin (distance: 11 miles).*

**Thursday, August 4:** *Arrive in Gennesaret (distance: 6 miles).*

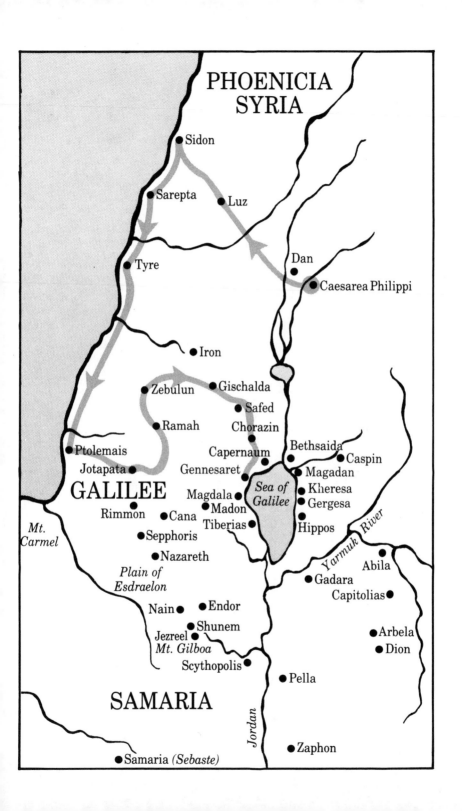

**A**fter the Capernaum crisis, the Pharisaic commissioners of the Jerusalem Sanhedrin were convinced that Jesus must be apprehended on a charge of blasphemy, or on one of flouting the sacred law of the Jews.

Until these charges could be drawn up and witnesses found to collaborate them, the decree to close all synagogues of Palestine to him would remain in effect. This was to be an unprecedented usurpation of authority by the Jerusalem Sanhedrin.

In the middle of May, a conference was held at Tiberias between the authorities at Jerusalem and Herod Antipas. The outcome of this conference was an agreement between Herod and the Sanhedrin representatives that Jesus should be seized and transported to Jerusalem for trial before the Sanhedrin, on charges of flouting the sacred laws of the Jewish nation. Accordingly, Herod signed the decree which authorized the officers of the Sanhedrin to seize Jesus.

Early the next morning, one of David Zebedee's messengers arrived at Jesus' camp bringing to him the news of Herod's decree, and saying that a number of Sanhedrin officers were, that very hour, on their way to arrest him with authority to take him to Jerusalem for trial.

Jesus well knew his hour had not yet come, and he would continue to teach and preach for almost another full year. Nevertheless, he thought it the wiser course of action to leave Bethsaida, never again to make his home at the house of Zebedee.

From this point on, the Master truly "had nowhere to lay his head." For the remainder of his life on the planet, he would never have a place to call home.

But Jesus had much work to do and he directed the apostles that they should embark immediately for Caesarea-Philippi, in Philip's domain, where they would be safe to continue preaching the gospel.

For the next two weeks, Jesus and his apostles would sojourn in the region of Caesarea-Philippi before leaving for the Phoenician coast in early June.

The Phoenicians were the first people to use the mode of crucifixion as a means of execution. These were also the last people to surrender the idea of sacrificing their first-born to their numerous tribal gods. It was to their god, Moloch, "the terrible god," to whom the Phoenicians offered living children as burnt sacrifices at Carthage, during the seige of the city. In 307 BC, 200 boys of the best families were burned to death on the altar to appease Moloch's wrath.

The Phoenicians, along with the Jews, especially revered the serpent, considering it to be the mouthpiece of evil spirits.

For Jesus and his apostles, their mission would remain the same, that of "thawing out the frozen forms of religion into the liquid liberties of enlightened sonship."

On Thursday morning, June 9, Jesus, his apostles and the evangelists left Caesarea-Philippi to begin their journey to the Phoenician coast. Their initial destination was Sidon, and so they headed for Luz, passing around the marsh country, until they reached the point of junction with the Magdala-Mount Lebanon trail road, and from there eventually crossing with the road leading to Sidon, arriving late afternoon the next day.

Referred to as the "Great Sidon" in the Old Testament, this remarkable Phoenician seaport on the eastern Mediterranean, was famous for its glass and bronze. These Phoenicians were the first of the middle-eastern people to establish relations with the ancient Greeks. Caravans from three continents traded here as they headed for the bazaars of Damascus and the markets of Rome.

It had been a two-day journey for Jesus and his 24 followers and when they arrived at the outskirts of Sidon, they stopped at the home of a well-to-do woman named Karuska, formerly of Bethsaida and a good friend of the Zebedee family.

Upon arriving at Karuska's home, Jesus instructed the apostles that he desired to rest and to tell no one of his presence.

Although the apostles obeyed Jesus' instructions, there was a servant girl who had taken the liberty to leave Karuska's house to tell a neighbor of Jesus' presence. This neighbor, Norana, was a Syrian woman who had a daughter about twelve years old, afflicted with a nervous disorder characterized by convulsions and other distressing manifestations. Norana had heard much of Jesus' teachings and healings and on this Sabbath afternoon she took her afflicted daughter to Jesus to be healed. (Matthew 15:22, Mark 7:25-26)

Upon arriving at the home of Karuska, she was met first by the Alpheus brothers — James and Judas — who explained that the Master was resting and could not be disturbed. Unperturbed, Norana replied that she and her daughter would remain right there until Jesus had finished his rest.

Simon Peter then interceded, explaining to Norana that Jesus was weary from much teaching and healing and that he had come to Phoenicia for a period of quiet and rest. But to Peter's chagrin, Norana only replied that she would not leave until she and her daughter had seen the Master.

Then Thomas tried to reason with her, but she rebuked him in a like manner, telling Thomas she had complete faith in Jesus to cast out this demon which tormented her child. To this Thomas replied, *Send her away, for she is shouting at us.* (Matthew 15:23)

Then came forward Simon Zelotes to remonstrate with this Greek-speaking gentile whom he held in great disdain. And Simon told her that she should not expect the Master to take

**87**

the bread intended for the children of the favored household and cast it to the dogs. (Matthew 15:26) But Norana paid little attention to Simon's insult, only to say that she understood his words to mean that she was only a dog in the eyes of the Jews, but as concerns Jesus, she was a believing dog. She had made up her mind that if Jesus would only look upon her daughter, he would heal her. Said Norana, *Even you would not dare to deprive the dogs of the privilege of obtaining the crumbs which fall from the children's table.* (Matthew 15:27, Mark 7:28)

Jesus, having heard all the commotion from an opened window, walked into the outer room about the same time the little girl was seized with violent convulsions, and Norana cried out, *Have mercy upon me, O Lord, Son of David; my daughter is cruelly demon-possessed.* (Matthew 15:22)

And Jesus said, *O woman, your faith is great, so great that I cannot withhold that which you desire; go your way in peace,* and the daughter was healed at once. (Matthew 15:28)

And Jesus told them to tell no one of this occurrence, but Norana, in her excitement, proclaimed her daughter's healing to the whole countryside, even in the town of Sidon.

As the word spread of this healing, the apostolic party, in order to avoid the miracle seekers once again, uprooted themselves this time to the home of Justa and her mother, Bernice, just north of the city of Sidon.

The apostles and the evangelists were spiritually uplifted by the manner in which the Gentiles of Sidon received them during their short stay in Phoenicia. This six-week period was a very fruitful time in terms of winning souls for the kingdom, as in many ways these Gentile believers were more open and receptive to Jesus' teachings than the Jews. These so-called heathens could more easily grasp the Master's teachings that God was no respecter of persons, races or nations and that there was no favoritism with the Universal Father. (Acts 10:34-35, Romans 2:11) Jesus was no threat to them and they openly received the truths of his teachings. In fact, it was here at Sidon, in the home of Justa, where Jesus told his disciples that, *Even though heaven and earth shall pass away, my words of truth shall not.* (Matthew 24:35, Mark 13:31, Luke 3:13-14)

It was at Sidon that the Master taught his disciples to go forward in righteousness or retrogress into evil and sin. They were told to *forget those things which are in the past while you push forward to what lies ahead.* (Philippians 3:13-14) And not only cease to do evil, but learn to do well. *If we confess our sins, he is faithful and just to forgive us our sins, and to cleanse us from all unrighteousness.* (I John 1:9) These disciples were told if they confessed their sins, they were forgiven, in that way to maintain a conscious void of offense before God and man. (Acts 24:16)

These Gentiles possessed a great sense of humor, in contrast to the burdensome religion of the Pharisees, which was void of all humor. Unlike these fun-loving Gentiles, the Jews in Jesus' day, especially the religious leaders, took themselves too seriously; *They strain at gnats and swallow camels,* Jesus said of them. (Matthew 23:24)

These Phoenician Gentiles spoke the Greek language, the majority of which descended from earlier Canaanite tribes of still earlier Semitic origin.

They were a great morale builder for the apostles and the evangelists, as they eagerly took to the gospel of the kingdom and became wholehearted believers.

On Sunday morning, Jesus and the apostles and evangelists left the home of Justa for the city of Tyre, heading down the coast by way of Sarepta, arriving late the following afternoon.

As famous as the Cedar of Lebanon was the purple dye of Tyre. Silk was so common during these times that men as well as women wore it. Silk and linen were colored with costly dyes and Romans would pay as much as a thousand denarii for a pound of double-dyed Tyrian wool. It was this industry and its purple dye from certain shellfish — the murex sea snail — that would make Tyre and Sidon famous the world over.

Tyre was the greatest of the Phonecian cities, built upon an island several miles off the coast. Under the reign of Alexander, Tyre was connected with the mainland by a wide causeway or mole, effectively making it a peninsula. Its splendid harbor and its security from attack made it the metropolis of Phoenicia, "a cosmopolitan bedlam of merchants and slaves from the whole Mediterranean world." It was a vast city with taller buildings than those of Rome and housed worse slums. There was a distinct odor, a product of the city's dying establishments, that permeated the town.

Over the years, Tyre had managed to survive sieges by Shalmaneser, Nebuchadnezzar, and Alexander, and by the time of Jesus' coming, many of its wealthy citizens had long since moved to Carthage to establish new centers of Phoenician trade.

Not long after Jesus' sojourn, the shellfish source of Tyrian dye would rapidly diminish, forcing the dye makers to seek new habitats of shellfish in which to supply their dyes.

It was these dye makers who heard and received Jesus' gospel of the kingdom — the fatherhood of God and the brotherhood of man — who would soon spread it around as they searched the ends of the earth for new habitats of purple dye producing shellfish.

For a two-week period, each of the apostles took one of John's evangelists and two-by-two they taught and preached in all parts of Tyre. During this time, Jesus and his followers made their headquarters at the home of a Jew named Joseph, a believer, who lived several miles south of Tyre, not far from the tomb of Hiram, the king of Tyre, during the times of David and Solomon.

Jesus and his apostles and evangelists would enter the city by way of Alexander's mole to conduct small meetings each day, while returning to camp at Joseph's house each evening.

During his brief sojourn at Tyre, Jesus gave his only sermon in Melkarth temple, the site on which a Christian church would be built in subsequent years.

It was in this building that Jesus told his followers that they must build well the foundations for the growth of noble character and spiritual endowments. He told them to make sure that the intellectual and moral foundations of character are such as will adequately support the superstructure of the enlarging and ennobling spiritual nature. (Matthew 7:24-27, Luke 6:47-49)

These disciples were beginning to comprehend that the soil of the evolving soul is human and material, but the destiny of the combined human mind and spirit is spiritual and divine.

They were learning that although men are led into temptation by the urge of their own selfishness and animal impulses, they must recognize temptation honestly and sincerely for just what it is, and intelligently redirect the energies of spirit, mind and body into higher channels and toward more idealistic goals. In order to yield the fruits of the spirit, they must be born of the spirit, Jesus was telling them.

Slowly, but surely, the message was sinking in: to seek God's will instead of supplanting one desire by another, supposedly superior, desire through mere force of the human will; that if they were to be triumphant over the temptations of the lesser and lower nature, they must be reborn of the spirit. In looking to God, they will in this way be delivered through spiritual transformation, rather than be increasingly overburdened with the deceptive suppression of mortal desires. (Ephesians 4:22-24) The old and the inferior will be forgotten in the love of the new and the superior, Jesus would tell them. (2 Corinthians 5:17, Colossians 3:9) And Jesus told them, in effect, that beauty is always triumphant over ugliness in the hearts of all who are illuminated by the love of truth. (Colossians 3:10) *Be not overcome by evil but rather overcome evil with good,* they were told. (Romans 12:21)

Gradually, the gospel of the kingdom was embedding itself in the minds of these disciples, that spiritual destiny is dependent on faith, love and devotion to truth — hunger and thirst for righteousness — the wholehearted desire to find God and to be like him. (Matthew 5:6, Luke 6:21) Their spiritual destiny would be conditioned only by their spiritual longings and purpose.

They were destined to live a narrow and mean life if they were only to love those who loved them, as there was no reward in loving only those who loved you. (Matthew 5:46) These men (and later the apostle, Paul) would learn this day that the less love in any creature's nature the greater the love need, and the more does divine love seek to satisfy such need. Love is never self-seeking, and it cannot be self-bestowed. Divine love cannot be self-contained; it must be unselfishly bestowed. (1 Corinthians 13:1-8)

As kingdom builders, they were learning that they must be undoubting of the truth of the gospel of eternal salvation; "that believers must increasingly learn how to step aside from the rush of life — escape the harassments of material existence — while they refresh the soul, inspire the mind, and renew the spirit by worshipped communion."

Every day a true believer lives, he finds it easier to do the right thing. The true believer does not grow weary in well-being just because he is thwarted. (2 Thessalonians 3:13) And let us not lose heart in doing good, for in due time we shall reap, if we do not grow weary. (Galatians 6:9)

This was a memorable sermon, and one not to be soon forgotten by these student-teachers, as they were learning this day to, *Render unto Caesar the things that are material and to God those which are spiritual.* (Matthew 22:21, Mark 12:17, Luke 10:25) They were learning that the measure of the spiritual capacity for the evolving soul is one's faith in truth and one's love for his fellow man.

These were but a few of the many things Jesus taught his associates that afternoon in the summer of AD 29.

It was approaching noon on Sunday, when Jesus and his apostles bid farewell to the evangelists who were directed to take a different route in their return to the region of the Sea of Galilee.

Jesus and the twelve apostles headed south along the coast to Ptolemais, and from there headed east to Jotapata, by way of the Tiberias road. The following day, the apostolic party headed north on the Nazareth-Mount Lebanon trail to the village of Zebulun, by way of Ramah.

Leaving Zebulun on Sunday, the last day of July, they journeyed over to the junction with the Magdala-Sidon road near Gischalda, and from there made their way to Gennesaret on the western shores of the sea of Galilee.

In this region, Jesus and his apostles could rest and teach, without fear of apprehension, before traveling back to Caesarea-Philippi the second week in August.

*Day 7:*

# **L**esson on Forgiveness

*(August 8 to August 19, Ad 29)*

# Lesson on Forgiveness
## 2 Week Period
### August 8-August 19, AD 29

**Monday, August 8:** *Apostles camped at Magadan Park, near Bethsaida-Julius. Jesus speaks to the hecklers. Beware of leaven of the Pharisees. (Matt. 16:6-12, Luke 12:1)*

**Tuesday, August 9:** *Apostolic party departs for Caesarea-Philippi, resting south of the waters of Merom. Jesus questions Apostles, Who do men say that I am? (Matt. 16:13, Mark 8:27, Luke 9:18) Arrive at home of Celsus in Caesarea-Philippi late evening (distance: 26 miles).*

**Thursday, August 11:** *Jesus speaks in Celsus' garden. I have come to seek and to save those who are lost. (Matt. 18:11, Mark 10:45) I have not come to call the righteous, but sinners. (Matt. 9:23, Mark 2:17, Luke 5:32) Before Abraham was, I am. (John 16:28) The Father and I are one. (John 10:30)*

**Monday, August 15:** *Jesus, Peter, James and John begin ascent of Mount Hermon. That evening, Peter, James and John witness Jesus' transfiguration. This is my beloved Son with whom I am well pleased; give heed to him. (Matt. 17:5, Mark 9:7) (distance: 12 miles)*

**Tuesday, August 16:** *Jesus, Peter, James and John arrive at camp at base of Mount Hermon. Jesus heals epileptic boy, casting out the demon. (Matt. 17:14-18, Mark 9:15-17, Luke 9:38-42)*

**Wednesday, August 17:** *Jesus and Apostles depart from Caesarea-Philippi for Magadan Park. Stop over at Simon Peter's in Capernaum, then to Magadan, arriving late evening (distance: 30 miles).*

**Friday, August 19:** *Beginning of Decapolis tour. Jesus teaches lesson on forgiveness at Hippos (distance: 8 miles). Not only seven times but seven times seventy. (Matt. 18:21, Luke 17:3-4) Freely have you received; freely give. (Matt. 10:8) Jesus tells parable about the king and his steward regarding mercy and forgiveness. (Matt. 18:21-35)*

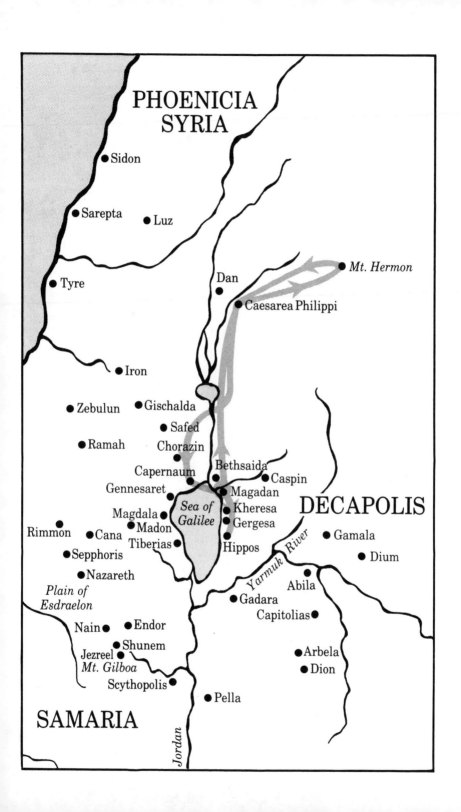

It had been almost three months since Jesus left Capernaum for the Phoenician Coast.

Having not seen him in Galilee since Herod signed the warrant for his arrest, Jesus' enemies concluded he would no longer be a threat to them.

The mandate to close all the synagogues to Jesus and his followers had backfired on the Jewish leaders. Having removed himself as an object of controversy, there gradually developed a strong resentment to the Pharisees and the Sanhedrin leaders at Jerusalem among the Jewish people. Even Philip, Herod's brother, having become a half-hearted believer in the teachings of Jesus, sent word to Jesus that he could live and teach in his domains.

Herod Antipas also sent word that, although he had signed warrants for Jesus' arrest in Galilee, he would not be apprehended in Perea as long as he remained outside Galilee.

The outward animosity toward the Jewish leaders by the Jewish people only served to intensify their pursuit of Jesus. Having discovered the Master's whereabouts on the shores of Lake Capernaum, they again sent out spies in hopes of entrapping him.

By this time, the Sadducees had joined the Pharisees in their effort to entrap Jesus.

On Monday, they found Jesus encamped in Magadan Park, near Bethsaida-Julias, with his apostles and evangelists and some 100 believers.

Before going to a closed conference with them, Jesus held a public meeting at which the Jewish leaders were present. It was their intention to disrupt the Master's teachings by heckling him and plying him with questions they hoped he could not answer, or would answer in a manner not in compliance with the laws of the elders.

With cunning intention, in front of the whole assembly, one of the leaders of the disturbers addressed the Master: "Teacher, we would like you to give us a sign of your authority to teach, and then, when the same shall come to pass, all men will know that you have been sent by God."

And Jesus answered them, *When it is evening you say it will be fair weather for the heaven is red; in the morning it will be foul weather for the heaven is red and lowering. When you see a cloud in the west you say showers will come; when the wind blows from the south you say scorching heat will come. How is it that you so well know how to discern the face of the heavens but are so utterly unable to discern the signs of the times? To those who would know the truth, already has a sign been given; but to an evil-minded and hypocritical generation no sign shall be given.* (Matthew 16:1-4, Mark 8:11, Luke 12:54-57)

After Jesus had spoken to these Jewish leaders, he and his followers broke from the assembly where he had more to say. *I say to you, beware of the leaven of the Pharisees and the Sadducees.* (Matthew 16:6-12, Mark 8:15, Luke 12:1) He told his followers not to be deceived by their show of much learning and by their profound loyalty to the forms of religion, to be only concerned with the spirit of living truth and the power of true religion. And they were further told that it was not the fear of a dead religion that would save them, but rather their faith in a living experience in the spiritual realities of the kingdom.

*Do not allow yourselves to become blinded by prejudice and paralyzed by fear, neither permit reverance for the tradition so to pervert your understanding that your eyes see not and your ears hear not.* (Mark 8:18)

These followers were learning that it is not the purpose of true religion merely to bring peace, but rather to ensure progress; that there can be no peace in the heart or progress in the mind unless one falls whole-heartedly in love with truth, the ideals of eternal realities. The issues of life and death were being set before all men — the sinful pleasures of time against the righteous realities of eternity. Jesus was telling them that they should strive to find deliverance from the bondage of fear and doubt as they entered upon the living of a new life of faith and hope.

The next morning, Tuesday, Jesus and the twelve set out from Magadon Park for Caesarea-Philippi, the capital of the Tetrach Philip's domain. Caesarea-Philippi was situated in a charming valley between scenic hills of wondrous beauty. In the middle of the valley, the river Jordan poured forth from an underground cave. In the background, one could view to the north the heights of Mount Hermon, and to the south a magnificent view of the upper Jordan and the Sea of Galilee.

The apostolic party journeyed south of the waters of Merom and since it was approaching noontime, they paused for lunch. As they sat under mulberry trees recalling their recent experiences in Phoenicia, Jesus confronted them with a surprising question. Said the Master, *Who do men say that I am?* (Matthew 16:13, Mark 8:27, Luke 9:18)

This shocking question provided considerable discussion among the apostles. Some said he was regarded as a prophet by all who knew him; others said that, although his enemies agreed he was an extraordinary man, they greatly feared him and felt he was in league with the prince of devils. Still others said that some in Judea and Samaria thought he was John the Baptist risen from the dead. Peter said he had heard him compared to Elijah, Jeremiah, and other prophets. (Matthew 16:14, Mark 8:28, Luke 9:19)

And then Jesus drew to his feet, and looking down upon them said, *But who do you think I am?* There was a moment of silence before Peter jumped to his feet exclaiming, *You are the Christ, the Son of the living God.* (Matthew 16:15-16, Mark

**99**

8:29, Luke 9:20)

Then Jesus beckoned Simon Peter to be seated, and while standing before them said, *This has been revealed to you by my Father. But for the time being I charge that you tell this to no man.* (Matthew 16:17, 20; Mark 8:30; Luke 9:21)

After lunch and a brief rest, Jesus and the twelve resumed their journey to Caesarea-Philippi, arriving late in the evening at the home of Celsus, who was expecting them.

It was noontime the following day when Jesus appeared before the apostles who were sitting in the garden about to prepare for lunch. During the lunch hour, Jesus and the twelve discussed their forthcoming tour of the Decapolis*, which would consume the better part of July and August. Soon after lunch, Jesus stood up and addressed his apostles, telling them that since they all believed he was the Son of the living God, he would upon this foundation build a brotherhood of the kingdom of heaven. Upon the rock of spiritual reality he would build the living temple of spiritual fellowship in the eternal realities of his Father's kingdom. (Matthew 16:18-20)

This confession of Peter that Jesus was the Son of God, a divine being, was not a part of the Jewish concept of the national deliverer — the Messiah. The Jews had not taught that the Messiah would spring from divinity. Although he was to be the "anointed one," he was hardly conceptualized to be the divine "Son of God." (Matthew 16:16; Mark 1:1, 8:29; Luke 9:20; John 1:34, 3:15-16)

For three years, Jesus had been proclaiming that he was the "Son of Man," while during this same period the apostles increasingly felt he was the expected Jewish Messiah. He now revealed to them he was the Son of God, and upon the concept of the combined nature of the Son of Man and the Son of God, he determined to build the kingdom of heaven. Jesus well knew it was futile to attempt to convince his apostles that he was not the Messiah — a king on the order of David — and so from this

---

*The region of Decapolis lying north of Perea and east of the Jordan with the exception of the city of Scythopolis was a confederation of ten cities. This land was acquired by the Greek conqueror, Alexander the Great, and later rulers of Egypt and Syria who governed the region encouraged Greek speaking peoples to colonize into ten cities; hence its name — Decapolis. In Jesus' day this region was governed by the ruler of Judea, subject to the emperor of Rome.*

point on he chose to reveal to them what he is, while ignoring their conceptualizations of his being the Messiah.

The next day was to be a very memorable day in the minds of the apostles, as Jesus was to teach them new truths, unfamiliar to them, about the kingdom of heaven.*

It was Thursday, August 11, and Jesus and the apostles would remain another day at the home of Celsus waiting for monies to arrive from David Zebedee. Ever since Jesus rejected the crown of David upon the feeding of the 5,000, financial support had fallen off, and by the time they reached Caesarea-Philippi, the treasury was nearly empty. Whenever the apostolic funds were low, Matthew always provided; and it was at this point he sold his last piece of property in Capernaum to sustain their ministry, directing that the proceeds be turned over to Judas.

David Zebedee had also undertaken the responsibility of providing funds to the apostles by sending messengers to Judea, Samaria, and Galilee to collect monies in support of Jesus and the 12.

It was while they were waiting for the Zebedee funds to arrive that Jesus spoke to his apostles in the garden of the Celsus home late that afternoon.

Standing before them, the Master said, *From this time on, if any man would have fellowship with us, let him assume the obligation of sonship and follow me. And when I am no more with you think not that the world will treat you better than it did your Master. If you love me, prepare to prove this affection by your willingness to take up the cross.* (Matthew 16:24, Mark 8:34, Luke 9:23)

*And mark well my words: I have not come to call the righteous, but sinners.* (Matthew 9:12-13, Mark 2:17, Luke 5:32) *The Son of Man came not to be ministered to but to minister and to bestow his life as the gift for all. I declare to you that I have come to seek and to save those who are lost.* (Matthew 18:11, 20:28; Mark 10:45)

*No man in this world now sees the Father except the Son*

---

*A new significance attaches to all of Jesus' teachings from this point on. Before Caesarea-Philippi, he presented the gospel of the kingdom as its master teacher. After Caesarea-Philippi, he appeared not merely as a teacher, but as the divine representative of the eternal Father — the son of God — acting in the capacity as a human being — the Son of Man.

*who came forth from the Father.* (Matthew 11:27, Luke 10:22, John 6:46) *But when the Son be lifted up, he will draw all men to himself and whosoever believes this truth shall be endowed with life that is everlasting.* (John 3:14-15, 12:32) *We may not yet proclaim openly that the Son of Man is the Son of God, but it has been revealed to you; wherefore do I speak truly to you concerning these mysteries. Though I stand before you in this physical presence, I came forth from God the Father. Before Abraham was, I am. I did come forth from the Father into this world as you have known me, and I declare to you that I must presently leave this world and return to the work of my Father.* (John 16:28, 8:58)

*My kingdom is not of this world. Can you believe the truth about me in the face of the fact that, though the foxes have holes and the birds of heaven have nests, I have not where to lay my head?* (Matthew 8:20, Luke 9:58, John 18:36)

*Nevertheless I tell you that the Father and I are one.* (John 10:30) *He who has seen me has seen the Father.* (John 14:9) *My Father is working with me in all these things and he will never leave me alone in my mission, even as I will never forsake you when you presently go forth to proclaim this gospel throughout the world.* (Hebrews 13:5)

Much of this information was new to the apostles, and they sat in stunned silence, as Jesus spoke so authoritatively about his sonship and his mission. They had confessed that he was the Son of God, but they were much confused as to what he wanted them to do.

Monday morning, August 15, Jesus, Peter and the Zebedee brothers — James and John — set out to ascend Mount Hermon. Of all the days in their association with Jesus, this day would bear witness to one of the most incredible incidents ever to take place on the planet — a celestial visitation with the Son of God — witnessed as it was by three mortals of the realm.

As if heaven opened before them, these three apostles received a fleeting glimpse of a celestial pageant, observing their Lord transfigured in glory before their very eyes. They could only stare in transfixed astonishment as the indelible word of God embedded itself upon the tablets of their minds. *This is my beloved Son with whom I am well pleased; give heed to him!* (Matthew 17:5, Mark 9:7)

This whole episode lasted but a few moments. Nevertheless

it would have a profound influence upon these apostles for the rest of their lives. It was a silent and pensive trio that accompanied Jesus down the slopes of Mount Hermon in the early hours that mid-August morning. No one spoke a word until Jesus said, *Tell no man what you have seen or heard on this mountain until the Son of Man has risen from the dead.* (Matthew 17:9, Mark 9:9)

Risen from the dead! What is he talking about, they pondered. The thought of Jesus dying was so distasteful to Peter, that he chose to change the subject to scriptural predictions of Elijah's return. In the back of their minds, however, Peter and the Zebedee brothers could not escape the thought that something dreadful might be in store for the Master.

Shortly before breakfast time, Jesus and his companions arrived at their camp at the base of Mt. Hermon. While they were away, a father, James of Safed, had set out to confront Jesus regarding the epileptic seizures of his fourteen-year-old son. The youth, although beset by terrible seizures, was also thought to be demon-possessed. Although the remaining nine apostles tried in vain to cast out this demon, their efforts ended in failure and humiliation.

When Jesus drew near, the anxious father approached him, and kneeling at his feet said, *Master, I have a son, an only child, who is possessed by an evil spirit causing him to scream, convulse, grit his teeth and foam at the mouth. He often falls into the fire and into the water.* (Matthew 17:15)

Jesus, looking about the score of skeptics that had followed James, rebuked these unbelievers saying, *O faithless and perverse generation, how long shall I bear with you? How long shall I put up with you?* And then pointing to the bewildered father he said, *Bring your son to me,* and when the boy was brought before him, the Master inquired of James, *How long has the lad been afflicted this way?* The father answered, *Since early childhood.* (Matthew 17:17, Mark 9:19-21, Luke 9:41)

As the two were talking, the young man was suddenly seized with a violent attack and fell before Jesus, gnashing his teeth and foaming at the mouth. After a succession of violent convulsions, he lay prostrate before the Master. The father again knelt before Jesus beseeching him to have compassion on his son. Said James, *Take pity on us; help us and deliver us from this terrible affliction.* And Jesus, bending down, looked into the eyes of James and said, *All things are possible to him who really believes.* (Mark 9:23) Then James of Safed spoke these memorable words of faith and doubt, *Lord, I believe. I pray you will help my unbelief.* (Mark 9:24)

When Jesus heard these words he stepped forward and taking the lad by the hand rebuked the unclean spirit saying, *Come out of him disobedient spirit and do not enter him again.* Then Jesus said, looking to the boy, *Arise my son,* and placing his hand in the hand of his father said, *Go your way, the Father has granted this desire of your soul.* (Matthew 17:18, Mark 9:25-27, Luke 9:42)

All those who witnessed this event, even the enemies of Jesus, were astonished at what they saw.

Early Wednesday morning Jesus and the 12 departed from Caesarea-Philippi for Magadan Park, near Bethsaida-Julias. Desiring to avoid the scribes and others who would soon follow them, the apostolic party journeyed south, and just beyond the waters of Merom they took the Damascus fork which passes through Galilee. (Mark 9:30)

This maneuver eluded the Master's enemies who reckoned he would take the east Jordan Road fearing to pass through the territory of Herod Antipas. The discussion as they journeyed toward Magadan Park centered not on the Master's latest miracle but instead on the destiny of the Son of Man.

Pausing along the Damascus Road to refresh themselves, Jesus addressed the twelve saying, *The Son of Man must presently go to Jerusalem, suffer many things, be rejected by the scribes, the elders, and the chief priests, and after all this, be killed and raised up on the third day. If anyone wishes to come after me, let him deny himself and take up his cross daily, and follow me. For whosoever would save his life selfishly, shall lose it, but whosoever loses his life for my sake and the gospels', shall save it. What does it profit a man to gain the whole world and lose his own soul? What would a man give in exchange for eternal life? Be not ashamed of me and my works in this sinful and hypocritical generation, even as I will not be ashamed to acknowledge you when in glory I appear before my Father in the presence of all the holy angels. Truly I say to you, many of you now standing before me shall not taste death till you see this Kingdom of God come with power.* (Matthew 16:21-28, Mark 8:31-38, Luke 9:22-27)

These sobering words were quite a shock to these Galilean fishermen who still persisted in dreaming of positions of honor for themselves in an earthly kingdom. Although they were beginning to grasp the idea about the possibility of the Master dying, his statement about rising from the dead failed to register in their minds.

In silence, they headed for their camp at Magadan Park, stopping at Simon Peter's house in Capernaum for an evening meal. Later that evening, David Zebedee sailed them across the lake to Magadan where they would immediately prepare for a month of teaching and preaching in the cities of the Decapolis.

In the course of a month, the apostles accompanied by almost 100 evangelists, would visit the cities of Gerasa, Gamala, Hippos, Zaphon, Gadara, Abila, Edrei, Philadelphia, Heshbon, Dion, Scythopolis, as well as a number of smaller towns.

There were no miracles associated with the Decapolis mission. Nevertheless, the apostles and their associated evangelists assimilated much of the spiritual teachings of Jesus' gospel of the kingdom. They would learn from the Master that *The Kingdom of God is within you.* (Luke 17:21); that many hungry souls would famish in the very presence of the bread of life and die searching for the very God who lives within them. In spite of living within the immediate grasp of living faith, such men would walk the earth seeking the treasury of the kingdom with yearning hearts and weary feet.

Jesus taught them that faith is to religion what sails are to a ship; an addition of power, not an added burden of life. *The gospel yoke is easy and the burden of truth is light,* he would tell them. (Matthew 11:29-30) Although Jesus never promised to deliver his apostles from the waters of adversity, he did promise to accompany them during such travail.

These apostles/evangelists were learning that in preaching the gospel, they were simply teaching friendship with God. And, although other religions had taught the nearness of God to man, Jesus personalized the Father's care much like that of a loving father to his dependent children. The worship of God and the service of man became the sum and substance of his religion.

The gospel of the kingdom was not to be passive and retiring but active and inspiring. Jesus took the passive doctrines of the Jewish religion and infused the spirit of positive action into them, making his new religion one of dynamic service in

105

the human brotherhood in contrast to passive compliance with the ancient laws. It required doing, as well as believing, those things which the gospel required. It was a religion that gave new insight to the elemental needs of the soul, one that required only a living faith in God. And such a faith they would learn will expand the mind, ennoble the soul, reinforce the personality, augment happiness, deepen the spirit perception, and enhance the power to love and to be loved.

One of the great lessons the apostles and the evangelists would learn had to do with forgiveness. It was early evening, Friday, the 19th of August, as Jesus and his apostles sat around the fire at their campsite at Hippos on the eastern shores of the Sea of Galilee. In answer to a disciple's question, Jesus said, *What do you think if a kind-hearted man has 100 sheep and one of them goes astray, does he not leave the 99 and go out in search of the one that has gone astray? And then, when the shepherd has found his lost sheep, he lays it over his shoulders and, going home rejoicing, calls to his friends and neighbors, 'Rejoice with me, for I have found my sheep that was lost.' I declare that there is more joy in heaven over one sinner who repents than over 99 righteous persons who need no repentance. Even so, it is not the will of my Father in heaven that one of these little ones should go astray, much less that they should perish.* (Matthew 18:12-14, Luke 15:3-7)

The lesson they were learning was that in their religion God may receive repentant sinners, but in the gospel of the kingdom the Father goes forth to find them even before they have seriously thought of repentance. For the Father in heaven loves his children and, therefore, they should learn to love one another; the Father in heaven forgives his children of their sins, therefore, they should learn to forgive one another.

*If your brother sins against you, go to him and reprove him in private and if he listens to you, you have won your brother. But if your brother will not hear you, if he persists in the error of his way, go again to him, taking with you two or three mutual friends as witnesses to confirm your testimony and establish the fact that you have dealt justly and mercifully with your offending brother. And if he refuses to hear your brothers, you may tell the whole story to the congregation and if he still refuses to hear the brotherhood, let such an unruly member become an outcast from the Kingdom.*

*Truly I say to you, whatsoever you shall decree on earth shall be recognized in heaven. Again I say to you, that if two of you agree on earth it shall be done for you if your petition is not inconsistent with the will of my Father in heaven. For where two or three have gathered together in my name there am I in the midst of them.* (Matthew 18:18-20)

Simon Peter, more often than not, a man of sudden impulse, lacking the sagacity of his older brother, asked one of his more thoughtless questions. *Lord, how often shall my brother sin against me and I forgive him? Up to seven times?* And Jesus answered Peter, *Not only seven times but seventy times seven. Therefore may the Kingdom of Heaven be likened to a certain king who ordered a financial reckoning with his stewards. And when he began to conduct this examination of accounts, one steward was brought to him confessing that he owed his king 10,000 talents. Pleading that he did not have the means to repay his lord, the king commanded that his property be confiscated and that he, his wife and children be sold to settle his debt. When the steward heard this stern decree, he prostrated himself before him saying, 'Lord have more patience with me, and I will pay you all.' And when the king looked upon this negligent servant and his family he was moved with compassion. He ordered the servant to be released and forgave him the debt.* (Matthew 18:21-27)

*And this steward, having thus received money and forgiveness at the hands of his king, went out and found a subordinate who owed him a mere 100 denarie, and seized him by the throat saying, 'Pay back what you owe me.' And then did this fellow steward fall before him and began to entreat him saying, 'Have patience with me and I will repay you.' But the chief steward would not show mercy to his fellow steward and had him thrown in prison until he could pay back his debt. When his fellow servants saw what had happened, they were so distressed that they went and told their lord — the king — what had happened. When the king heard of the doings of his chief steward, he called this ungrateful and unforgiving man before him and said, 'You are a wicked and unworthy steward. When you sought compassion, I freely forgave you your entire debt. Should you not have also had mercy on your fellow servant, even as I had mercy on you?' And his lord moved with anger, handed the ungrateful steward over to the jailers that they might hold him until he paid all that was due. And even so shall my heavenly Father show the* more abundant mercy to those who freely show mercy to their fellows." (Matthew 18:28-35)

It was a lesson on human compassion and forgiveness. How could one come to God asking consideration for his shortcomings when he is wont to chastise his brethren for being guilty of the same human frailties? Thus did Jesus teach the dangers and the unfairness of sitting in personal judgment upon one's fellows.

Then said the Master, "Freely you have received the good things of the kingdom, therefore, freely give to your fellows on earth." (Matthew 10:8)

It was now late in the evening on this warm summer night, and the apostles and their fellow evangelists had much to ponder as they bedded down for the night.

*Day 8:*

# he Feast of Tabernacles

*(September 26 to October 6, AD 29)*

# The Feast of the Tabernacles
## 10 Day Period
### September 26 to October 6, AD 29

**Monday, September 26:** *Jesus and his Apostles leave Magadan, passing down the eastern shore of the lake camping east of Scythopolis (distance: 26 miles).*

**Tuesday, September 27:** *Encounter with Samaritan on eastern slopes of Mt. Gilboa. James and John, the "Sons of Thunder," ask permission to bring fire down from heaven to devour the Samaritans. (Luke 9:51-56)*

**Wednesday, September 28:** *Arrive in Bethany late evening (distance: 52 miles). Jesus teaches at the temple. I know the Father, for I have come from the Father to declare and reveal him to you. (John 7:27-29) Nothing will befall the Son of Man until his hour has come. (John 7:30) I have come that you may have life and have it eternally. (John 3:15) In a short time I go to Him who sent me into this world. (John 7:33) I am the light of the world. (John 8:12) You shall know the truth and the truth shall make you free. (John 8:32) Before Abraham was, I am. (John 8:58)*

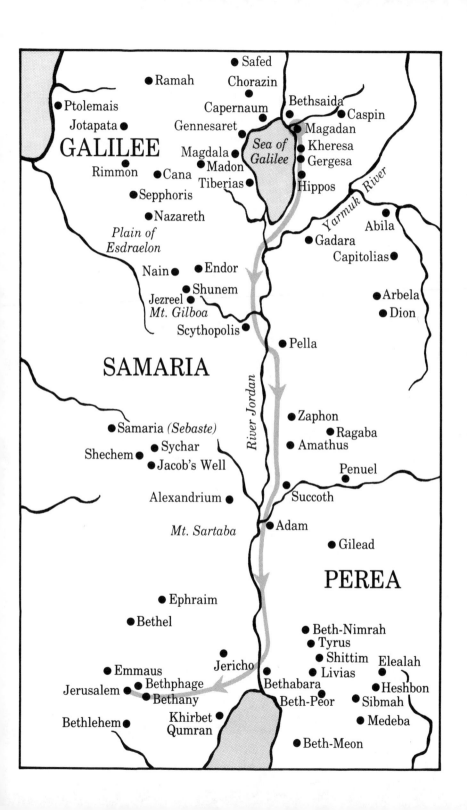

**A**fter some four weeks of teaching in the Decapolis, Jesus and his apostles arrived at Magadan Park for a week of rest in mid-September. The Decapolis mission had been moderately successful for the apostles and evangelists, having received hundreds of souls into the kingdom.

Now they would relax a while before making plans to visit Perea, east of the Jordan, early the next year. This was to be their last sustained rest, as the Perean tour would extend right on down to the time of their arrival in Jerusalem for the Passover and the Master's arrest.

While the apostles rested, others made plans in support of their upcoming mission. Abner, the head of the 70 evangelists, moved his base of operations from Hebron to Bethlehem, where David Zebedee headquartered his messenger service in Judea. There, messengers kept believers throughout Palestine in touch with one another, as well as serving as collectors of funds to not only sustain the apostolic corps but their families as well.

After a long week's rest, Jesus announced they would attend the Feast of Tabernacles in Jerusalem the following week.

The Feast of Tabernacles was the feast of harvest ingathering, and coming as it did in the cool of the autumn months, it was more generally attended by the Jews of the world than was the Passover at the end of the winter, or Pentecost at the beginning of summer.

People from all over the known world as far as Spain and India would come to Jerusalem to participate in these autumn festivities. They would live in the open air, in leafy booths. It was a season of vacation pleasures coupled with the solemn rites of religious worship, a time of racial rejoicing, mingled with sacrifices and ritual ceremonies.

The entire city was gaily decorated, except the Roman fortress of Antonia, which was a grim reminder of Roman suzerainty. At night, the temple was brilliantly illuminated by the great candelabras which burned brightly in the women's court, as well as the myriad of torches standing about the temple courts.

This Feast of Tabernacles was considered the feast of feasts, since any sacrifice not made at the other festivals could be made at this time.

It was early Monday morning, September 26, when Jesus and his apostles set out for Jerusalem, by way of the heathen city, Scythopolis, inside the borders of Samaria. In the early afternoon, Jesus sent Philip and Matthew over to the village on the eastern slopes of Mount Gilboa to secure lodging for the party.

Now, these Samaritan villagers hated the Jews as much as the Jews hated them, and they refused Philip and Matthew lodging because they heard that Jesus and his associates were Jews.

Upon hearing the indignities heaped upon Philip and Matthew when they returned, James and John stepped up to Jesus and said, *Master, shall we bid fire come down from heaven to devour these insolent and impertinent Samaritans.* But when Jesus heard these words of vengeance, he turned on the "sons of thunder" and severely rebuked them. (Luke 9:51-56)

And so, that evening, Jesus and his apostles stopped over at a village near the Jordan ford. Early the next morning, they continued on to Jerusalem, crossing the Jordan and traveling along the east Jordan highway, arriving at Bethany late Wednesday evening. They were to stay in this vicinity near Jerusalem until the end of October, a period of just over one month.

The apostles knew the Jewish authorities were just waiting for the right moment to arrest Jesus and, for this reason, they feared to enter Jerusalem. Jesus' followers also knew the Sanhedrin had their spies looking for Jesus, and everyone was surprised beyond belief when the Master showed up in the temple to teach. The multitudes who had heard him speak and teach were of divided opinion. Some said he was a good man, while others said he led people astray with his strange doctrines. His friends feared to acknowledge him openly for fear of the Jewish leaders, while his enemies hesitated to denounce him openly for fear of the overwhelmig support of the multitudes. But everyone marveled at his teaching, knowing he had not been instructed in the schools of the rabbis. (John 7:11-15)

The temple was located in the north-eastern section of the city and shared a common wall on the northwest side with the Antonia fortress. On the eastern and southern boundaries were narrow porches, formed by tall columns, which housed the teaching scribes, the merchants and the money changers. This large open area was called the court of the Gentiles and opened to anyone.

Along the back of this courtyard were the many cages holding the various sacrificial animals, depending on what one could afford, ranging in size from doves to oxen.

There were several levels to the court, the first of which was a central gathering place for the Jews. Fifteen steps above that was the Court of Women housing a number of trumpet-shaped containers for money offers. Above the women's court hung the Nicanor gate, huge bronze doors that took as many as 20 men to open and close.

Up through more steps and separated by a railing was the Court of Priests. Towards the front of this court stood the altar and behind it the temple which was built of white marble with gold trim around the top.

Immediately behind the altar stood the priest and Levites

who worked barefooted on a platform, as water and blood were always on the floor.

The Levites did most of the work and could be recognized by their bright yellow robes. The priests were distinguished by their white coats with wide sashes that wrapped around their waist three times and by cone-shaped hats. Their shawls were a striped white and brown.

The Feast of Tabernacles was the busiest time of year for these men, performing as they did more sacrifices than at any other feasts.

During the feast, 70 bullocks would be sacrificed, symbolically representing the 70 nations of heathendom.

It was after this ritual sacrificing of some of these animals that Jesus first spoke in the temple. No sooner than he began was he interrupted by a curious listener who asked, *Teacher, how is it you can quote the Scriptures and teach the people so fluently when I am told you are untaught in the learning of the rabbis?* And Jesus replied: *No man has taught me the truths which I declare to you. And this teaching is not mine but his who sent me. If any man really desires to do my Father's will, he shall certainly know about my teaching, whether it be God's or whether I speak for myself. He who speaks for himself seeks his own glory, but when I declare the words of the Father, I thereby seek the glory of him who sent me. Did Moses not give you the law, yet how many of you honestly seek to fulfill its demands? Moses in the law enjoins you, saying 'You shall not kill'; notwithstanding this command some of you seek to kill the Son of Man.* (John 7:14-19)

When the multitude heard these words, they began arguing among themselves. Some said he was indeed the prophet of Galilee whom the scribes and Pharisees sought to kill, while others said he possessed a demon. After some discussion, one man from the crowd stepped forward and asked Jesus, *Why do the rulers seek to kill you?* and he replied: *The rulers seek to kill me because they resent my teaching about the good news of the kingdom, a gospel that sets man free from the burdensome traditions of a formal religion of ceremonies which these teachers are determined to uphold at any cost. They circumcise in accordance with the law of Moses on the Sabbath Day, but they would kill me because I once set free a man held in the bondage of affliction and made him completely whole on the Sabbath Day.* (John 7:21-23)

Many could recognize the hypocrisy in these religious leaders. They recognized that these leaders sought to kill Jesus because they well knew that if they honestly believed and dared to accept his teachings, their system of traditional religion would be overthrown and forever destroyed. Jesus' new gospel of the kingdom of God was a direct threat to those learned men and would jeopardize their authority over the people. And Jesus said to them: *Judge not according to outward appearances but rather judge by the true spirit of these teachings; judge righteously.* (John 7:24)

Then another man asked, *Do you really claim to be the Messiah?* And Jesus replied *You claim to know me and to know whence I am. I wish your claims were true, for indeed, then would you find abundant life in that knowledge. But I declare that I have not come to you for myself; I have been sent by the Father, and he who sent me is true and faithful. By refusing to hear me, you are refusing to receive him who sends me. You, if you will receive this gospel, shall come to know him who sent me. I know the Father, for I have come from the Father to declare and reveal him to you.* (John 7:27-29)

Never had these Pharisees heard such a bold proclamation of sonship. Here in their temple, Jesus was announcing his divinity to all Jewry from all parts of the known world. This Galilean was assaulting their leadership and threatening their very purpose.

The agents of the scribes and Pharisees wanted to lay hands upon Jesus, but they feared the multitude, for many believed him. And they were saying, *Even though this teacher is from Galilee, and even though he does not meet all our expectations of the Messiah, we wonder if the deliverer, when he does come, will really do anything more wonderful than this Jesus of Nazareth has already done.* (John 7:30-31)

Now these Jewish leaders were quite bewildered and befuddled at the Master's boldness in apparently flouting their leadership. Competition they did not need, especially since the competition was claiming to be of higher authority than even Abraham. Something had to be done to quiet Jesus, but what? Had he been secretly given immunity to teach by the Roman authorities? Otherwise how could he possibly be so assertive and bold in face of the threat of death? The Pharisees were certain Jesus was given immunity, but the officers of the Sanhedrin reasoned otherwise. They could not believe that the Romans would grant Jesus immunity from them, being a Jew himself, without the knowledge of the highest governing body of the Jewish nation.

Accordingly, after considerable discussion, they dispatched one Eber, an officer of the court, along with two assistants to arrest Jesus. As these men made their way towards Jesus, not wishing to interrupt him, they stopped short and listened to what he had to say. So impressed were they at his majestic appearance and the content of his message, they refused to carry out the order to arrest him. (John 7:32, 46)

Jesus was telling the assemblage that he had not come to bear ill will, that the Father loved them and, therefore, he longed for their deliverance from the bondage of prejudice and the darkness of tradition; that he came to offer them the liberty of life and the joy of salvation, and to proclaim the new and living way, the deliverance from evil and the breaking of the bondage of sin. Said Jesus, *I have come that you may have life, and have it eternally.* (John 3:15, 5:24-25, 39-40)

*If you could only realize that I am to be with you only a little while. In just a short time, I go to him who sent me into this world. And then will many of you seek me, but you shall not discover my presence, for where I am about to go you cannot come. But all who truly seek to find me shall sometime attain the life that leads to my Father's presence.* (John 7:33-34, 8:21)

And some of the skeptics said, *Where will this man go that we cannot find him? Will he go to live among the Greeks? Will he destroy himself? What can he mean when he declares that soon he will depart from us, and that we cannot go where he goes?* (John 7:35-36; 8:20)

Having heard Jesus speak, Eber and his fellow officers returned to the chief priests without arresting him. When upbraided for not bringing Jesus to them, Eber could only reply, *We have never heard a man speak like this man. You would all do well to go over and hear him.* When the chief rulers heard these words, they were astonished and sternly addressing Eber said, *Are you also lead astray? Are you about to believe in this deceiver? Have you heard that any of our learned men or any of the rulers have believed in him? Have any of the scribes or Pharisees been deceived by his clever teachings? How does it come that you are influenced by the behavior of this ignorant multitude who know not the law of the prophets? Do you not know that such untaught people are accursed?* (John 7:45-49)

Some of the Sanhedrin court were not so adverse to Jesus' teaching, while still others were secret followers. One of these believers, Nicodemus, spoke up, *But this man speaks to the multitudes words of mercy and hope. He cheers the downhearted, and his words were comforting even to our souls. What can there be wrong in these teachings even though he may not be the Messiah of the Scriptures? And even then does not our law require fairness? Do we condemn a man before we hear him?* And the chief of the Sanhedrin said to him, *Have you gone mad? Are you by any chance also from Galilee? Search the Scriptures and you will discover that out of Galilee arises no prophet, much less the Messiah.* (John 7:50-52)

The majority of this body were all the more convinced that Jesus was a transgressor of the law, a perverter of the people, and a menace to their authority, and had to be reckoned with as soon as possible. They would once more set out to entrap him or to discredit him with his followers, all the while hoping he would say something adversarial to Roman authority or to the Laws of Moses.

Now, although these scribes and Pharisees were spiritually blind and intellectually prejudiced by their loyalty to tradition, they were to be numbered among the more thoroughly moral men of that day and generation.

Adultery, to them, was a sin punishable by death, according to the Law of Moses, but under Roman authority they did not have the right to condemn their own, so they contrived a scheme that would put the Master in an uncompromising position.

As Jesus was teaching near the temple, he was met by a group of hired agents of the Sanhedrin who were dragging a woman along with them. As they approached him their spokesman said, *Teacher, this woman has been caught in adultery, in the very act. Now the Law of Moses commands that we should stone such a woman. What do you say should be done with her?* (John 8:2-5)

Jesus' enemies knew that if he upheld the Law of Moses requiring that the self-confessed transgressor be stoned, he would be violating Roman law which denied the right of the

Jews to inflict the death penalty. On the other hand, if he condemned such action they would accuse him before the Sanhedrin court of setting himself above Moses and the Jewish law. If, on the other hand, he chose to remain silent, they would accuse him of cowardice.

Jesus, knowing their nefarious intentions, handled the situation in such a manner that the whole scheme fell to pieces of its own sordid weight.

Under Jewish law there had to be a witness to such deprecation and Jesus, spotting the accuser — the woman's husband — who was a party to the despicable scheme, walked over to him, bent down and wrote in the sand, causing him to leave in great haste. Then Jesus came back to the woman saying, *He who is without sin among you, let him cast the first stone,* and once again for these would-be accusers, he bent down and wrote in the sand and when they read his words they too departed. Then Jesus turned to the woman and said, *Woman, where are your accusers? Did no man remain to stone you?* And she said, *No one, Lord.* And then Jesus said, *I know about you; neither do I condemn you. Go your way in peace.* (John 8:6-11) And this woman, Hildana, foresook her wicked husband and joined herself to the disciples of the kingdom.

Later on in the evening, against the brilliantly illuminated light of the candelabras and the torches of the temple, Jesus stood up in the midst of the people and said, *I am the light of the world. He who follows me shall not walk in darkness but shall have the light of life.* (John 8:12) But the Pharisees interrupted saying, *You bear witness to yourself but your witness is not true.* And Jesus answered, *Even if I do bear witness about myself, my witness is everlastingly true, for I know whence I came, who I am and whither I go. You who would kill the Son of Man, know not whence I came, who I am, or whither I go. You judge only by the appearance of the flesh; you do not perceive the realities of the spirit. I judge no man. But if I should choose to judge, my judgment would be true and righteous, for I would judge not alone, but in association with my Father, who sent me into the world and who is the source of all true judgment. You even allow that the witness of two reliable persons may be accepted — well then I bear witness to these truths; so also does my Father in heaven. And when I told you this yesterday, in your darkness you asked me 'Where is your Father?' Truly you know neither me nor my Father, for if you had known me, you would also have known my Father. I have already told you that I am going away and that you will seek me and not find me, for where I am going you cannot come. You who would reject this light are from beneath; I am from above. You who would prefer to sit in darkness are of this world; I am not of this world.* (John 7:33-34; 8:13-23)

*I am the light of life and everyone who deliberately rejects this saving light shall die in his sins. Much I have to tell you, but you are unable to receive my words. However, he who sent me is true and faithful; my Father loves even his erring children and all that my Father has spoken I also proclaim to the world.*

*When the Son of Man is lifted up then shall you all know that I am he, and that I have done nothing of myself but only as the Father has taught me. I speak these words to you and to your children, and he who sent me is even now with me; he has not left me alone for I do always that which is pleasing in his light.* And as Jesus spoke these words, many came to believe in him. (John 8:23-30)

On the last day of this feast, some 900 priests and Levites officiated in the ceremonies. Early in the morning, pilgrims assembled from all parts of the city, each carrying in the right hand a sheaf of myrtle, willow and palm branches, while in the left hand each one carried a branch of the paradise apple — the citron, or the "forbidden fruit." These pilgrims were separated into three groups. One group remained at the temple to attend the morning sacrifices; another group headed for Maza, south of Jerusalem, to cut the willow branches for adornment of the sacrificial altar, while the last group formed a procession to march from the temple behind the water priests, who to the sound of trumpets carried the golden pitchers of symbolic water, out through Ophel to near Siloam where the fountain gate was located. After filling the golden pitcher at the pool of Siloam, the procession marched back to the temple, entering by way of the water gate and heading directly to the court of the priests. Here the priest bearing the water pitcher was joined by the priest bearing the wine for the drink offering. Together they walked towards this altar and poured the contents into two silver funnels which led to the base of the altar.

The ceremony of the outpouring of the water symbolized the outpouring of the divine spirit. This ceremony of the water followed the sunrise procession of the priest and Levites. The worshippers passed down the steps leading from the court of Israel to the court of the women, while successive blasts were blown upon the silvery trumpets. And then the faithful marched on toward the beautiful gate, which opened upon the court of the Gentiles. Here they turned about to face westward, to repeat their chants, and to continue their march for the symbolic water.

The execution of this rite of pouring the wine and the water was the signal for the assembled pilgrims to begin the chanting of the Psalms from 113 to 118 inclusive, in alternation with the Levites. As they spoke the Psalm, they would wave their sheaves at the altar. Then followed the sacrifices for the day, associated with the repeating of the Psalm of that day.

On this last day, the great day of the feast, the procession from the pool of Siloam passed through the temple courts, following the priest with the holy water.

After the water and the wine had been poured down upon the altar by the priests, after the chanting of the Hallel and the responsive reading of the 82 Psalm beginning with verse five, there was a pause in the proceedings, as the priests prepared the sacrifices. During this interlude, Jesus, standing among the pilgrims said, *If any man thirst, let him come to me and drink. From the Father above I bring to this world the water of life. He who believes me shall be filled with the spirit which this water represents, for even the Scriptures have said, 'out of him shall flow rivers of living waters.' When the Son of Man has finished his work on earth, there shall be poured out upon all flesh the living spirit of truth. Those who received this spirit shall never know spiritual thirst.* (John 7:37-39)

When Jesus finished speaking, some thought he was a prophet, more thought him to be the Messiah, still others said he could not be the Christ, seeing that he came from Galilee, and that the Messiah must restore David's throne. Although some wanted to seize him, they dared not arrest him among his followers. (John 7:40-44)

Jesus was not yet through in his attempts to persuade the skeptics that spiritual freedom was available to all who chose to learn and follow God's word. He would try one last time to convince his enemies, those whose souls were sealed by prejudice and blinded by the pride of revenge, that he brought them truth which he received from the Father. Accordingly, on the afternoon of the last day of the feast, Jesus entered the temple and, finding a large group of believers assembled in Solomon's porch, he approached them saying: *If my words abide in you and you are reminded to do the will of my Father, then are you truly my disciples? You shall know the truth, and the truth shall make you free.* But one of the Pharisees interrupted him saying, *We are the children of Abraham and we are in bondage to none; how then shall we be made free?* This man could not comprehend that Jesus was not referring to the outward subjection to another's rule, but to the liberties of the soul. Said Jesus, in answer to this man's question, *Verily, verily, I say to you, everyone who commits sin is the bond servant of sin. And you know that the bond servant is not likely to abide forever in the Master's home. You also know that the Son does remain in the Father's house. If, therefore, the Son shall make you free, you shall be free indeed.* (John 8:31-36)

    *I know that you are Abraham's offspring, yet your leaders seek to kill me because my word has not been allowed to have its transforming influence in their hearts. I declare to you the truth which the eternal Father shows me, while these teachers seek to do the things which they have learned only from their temporal fathers.* Then another Pharisee spoke up saying, *Abraham is our Father.* And Jesus replied, *If you were the children of Abraham you would do the works of Abraham. Some of you believe my teaching but others seek to destroy me because I have told you the truth which I received from God. But Abraham did not so treat the truth of God.* (John 8:37-41)

    Then Jesus went on to say, *If God were your Father, you would know me and love the truth which I reveal. Will you not see that I come forth from the Father, that I am sent by God, for I have not come on my own initiative but by he who sent me. Why do you not understand my words? It is because you have become children of evil. If you are children of darkness you will hardly walk in the light of truth which I reveal. The children of evil follow only in the ways of their father, who was a deceiver and stood not for the truth because there come to be no truths in him. But now comes the Son of Man speaking and living the truth, and many of you refuse to believe.*

    *Which one of you convicts me of sin? If I, then, proclaim and live the truth shown me by the Father, why do you not believe me? He who is of God hears the words of God; for this reason many of you hear not my words, because you are not of God.*

Again a Pharisee yelled out, *Do we not say rightly that you are a Samaritan and have a demon?* And Jesus answered, *All of you who deal honestly with your own souls know full well that I do not have a demon. You know that I honor the Father even while you would dishonor me. I seek not my own glory, only the glory of my Father. And I do not judge you but does the Father.* (John 8:42-50)

It was the belief of these antagonists that their scriptures were infallible and that the word of the ancient authors was unassailable. They would just as soon believe that the god of love directed their forefathers to go forth in battle to slay all their enemies — men, women and children.

This prophet standing in their midst had no guts for conquest. He could hardly fill the shoes of an Abraham or a David. How could he lead them out of Roman bondage; only a Messiah on the order of King David could do that.

To these hardened Pharisees, truth had been revealed to another generation, and through their visions had forever embedded itself in holy Scripture. They just refused to believe that God does not limit truth to any one generation or to any one people, therefore, they could not see that living truth — the "Son of God" was in their midst. Jesus instead represented a threat to their established traditions.

Because of their rigid adherence to tradition, they could not fathom that the revelations of divine truth are not sealed except by human ignorance, bigotry and narrow-minded intolerance, "that the light of the Scriptures is only dimmed by prejudice and darkened by superstition."

Jesus was telling them that the authority of truth is the very spirit that dwells in living manifestation and not the dead words of the less illuminated and supposedly inspired men of another generation.

Said Jesus to these stubborn men, *Verily, verily I say to you who believe the gospel that if a man will keep this word of truth alive in his heart, he shall never taste death.* But certain unbelievers hollered, *Now we know you have a demon seeing that Abraham and the prophets are dead, and you say, 'If anyone keeps my word, he shall never taste death.' Are you so much greater than Abraham and the prophets that you dare to stand here and say that whom keeps your word shall not taste death?*

*Who do you claim to be that you utter such blasphemies.* And Jesus replied, *If I glorify myself, my glory is nothing. But it is the Father who shall glorify me even the same Father whom you call God. Though you know not the Father, I truly know him. Even Abraham rejoiced to see my day, and by faith he saw it and was glad.* (John 8:51-56)

By this time, many of the unbelieving agents of the Sanhedrin had gathered, and when they heard these words they chanted, "You are not fifty years of age, and yet you talk about seeing Abraham; you are a child of the devil!"

Unable to continue his discourse, Jesus turned to them as he departed, saying, *Verily, verily I say to you, before Abraham was, I am.* Many of the unbelievers rushed to pick up stones to throw at him, but before they could do so, Jesus had departed from the temple. (John 8:57-59)

This was the boldest proclamation of sonship the master's followers and his enemies had ever heard. It was of great spiritual comfort for these believers, but to the agents of the Sanhedrin, it was out and out blasphemy. And this blasphemy would be dealt with in a most expeditious and thorough manner.

# Day 9:

## abbath Sermon at Pella

### *(October 28 to January 28, AD 29-30)*

# Sabbath Sermon at Pella
3 Month Period
October 28 to January 28, AD 29-30

**Friday, October 23:** *Jesus leaves Bethany for Ephraim (distance: 14 miles).*

**Sunday, October 30:** *Jesus leaves Ephraim for Magadan. Arrives late afternoon, Wednesday, November 2 (distance: 64 miles). Here Jesus ordains the seventy evangelists to preach and teach, two by two, in the countryside. I am about to send you out as lambs among the wolves. (Luke 10:3) Be as wise as serpents while you are harmless as doves. (Matthew 10:16) Freely you received; freely give. (Matthew 10:8)*

**Tuesday, December 6:** *Jesus leaves Magadan for Pella in Perea (distance: 28 miles). Delivers sermon on The Good Shepherd. (John 10:1-18) I am the door; if anyone enters through me he should be saved. (John 10:9) Delivers sermon on Spiritual Preparedness. To the angels, the very hairs on your head are numbered. (Luke 12:7)*

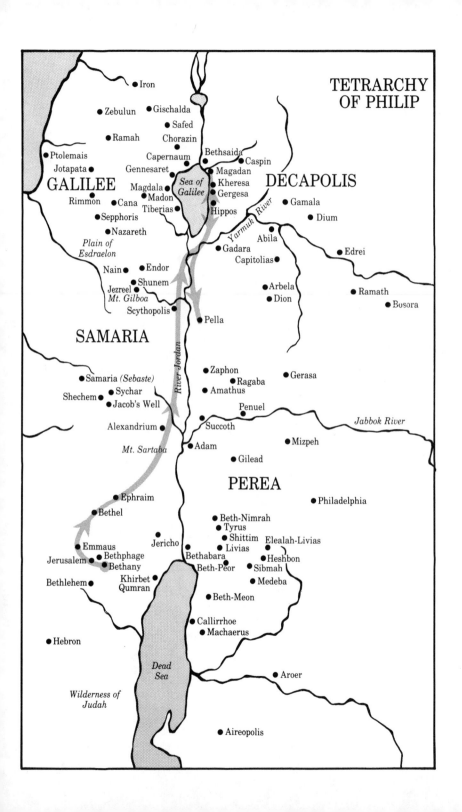

**S**oon after the great day of the feast, Jesus and the Apostles departed Jerusalem for their camp at Bethany where the Master spent some personal time with his friends, Lazarus, Martha and Mary. (Luke 10:38-39) There he and the twelve would tarry for the remainder of October teaching in the surrounding communities.

It was during this period of some thirty days that Jesus divided his time with his Apostles in Bethany and the many followers of John the Baptist under the leadership of Abner in Bethlehem.

In late October the apostolic party headed north by way of Ephraim and the west Jordan Highway, crossing the Jordan ford and arriving at Magadan on the northeastern shores of the Sea of Galilee late Wednesday afternoon, November 2, AD 29.

Soon after their arrival, Abner and seventy evangelists

met with them to be further instructed by Jesus in the gospel of the Kingdom. (Luke 10:1)

Much as his apostles were ordained some two years earlier, the seventy evangelists were soon to be ordained as gospel preachers and teachers in the service of the Kingdom.

Addressing the seventy at Magadan Park, Jesus said: *The harvest is plentiful, but the laborers are few; therefore, I exhort all of you to pray that the Lord of the harvest will send still other laborers into his harvest. I am about to send you out as lambs among wolves, therefore, be as wise as serpents while you are also harmless as doves. As you go your way, two by two, I instruct you to carry neither purse nor extra clothing for you go on this mission for only a short season. And whatever house you enter, first say, 'Peace be to this house.' If those who love peace live therein, you shall abide there. If not, then you shall depart. And stay in that house eating and drinking what they give you for the laborer is worthy of his wages. Do not keep moving from house to house. And everywhere you go heal those who are sick and say to them: 'The Kingdom of heaven is at hand.' Freely have you received of the good things of the Kingdom; freely give.* (Matthew 10:7-16, Luke 10:2-9)

Then as the seventy knelt before the Master, the Son of God looked down upon these humble men and said: *He who hears you hears me; and he who hears me hears him who sent me. He who rejects me rejects him who sent me.* (Luke 10:16)

It was an exhilarating moment for these soon to be God's messengers, and they immediately set out visiting the cities of Galilee, Samaria and Judea preaching and teaching, two by two, the gospel as they understood it.

These seventy disciples would continue to preach for about six weeks until they again met up with Jesus and his apostles at Pella in Perea the first of the year.

In early January, AD 30, Abner, former head of the followers of John the Baptist, now chief to the seventy messengers of the kingdom, called his associates together for a final tour. This Perean mission would last for almost three months as the seventy evangelists working alongside Jesus and his apostles would minister to some sixty cities, villages and towns including Zaphon, Arbela, Ramath, Endrei, Bosora, Caspin, Gerasa, Amathus, Adam, Capitolias, Dion, Philadelphia, Gilead, Beth-Nimrah, Livias, Heshbon, Sibmah, Medeba, Areopolis and Aroer, to name but a few.

Perea, at this time, was the most beautiful and picturesque province in all Palestine and was generally referred to by the Jews as "the land beyond the Jordan." Perea was divided about equally between Gentile and Jew, as many of the Jews had been dispersed during the times of Judas Maccabee.

During this period from January to March, Jesus divided his time between his camp at Pella and his periodic visits to assist these evangelists and apostles in their teaching. No other part of Palestine was so thoroughly worked by Jesus' apostles/ disciples than this region and these people were very receptive to the Master's teaching.

By mid-January, over 1,000 people had gathered together at Pella, where Jesus taught at least once each day, usually speaking in the mornings, while Peter and the other apostles taught in the afternoon. The evenings were usually reserved for open discussion consisting of questions and answers. There was little field work attempted by the twelve, allowing Abner and his associates to do most of the teaching and baptizing.

Saturday, January 28, was to be a memorable afternoon, as Jesus was about to preach a sermon on "Trust and Spiritual Preparedness" to some 3,000 believers.

The night before, Jesus had spoken to a group of 100 followers, as well as a number of Pharisees, on the subject of "The Good Shepherd." In this sermon, he told them that through this life in the flesh he was about to judge both the false shepherds and the true shepherds.

He iterated that *If you were blind, you would have no sin, but you claim that you see; you profess to be teachers in Israel; therefore, does your sin remain upon you.* (John 9:41)

He further told them that the true shepherd gathers his flock into the fold for the night in times of danger. And when the morning comes, he enters into the fold by the door; and when he calls them, they know him by his voice. Every shepherd who gains entrance to the sheepfold by any other means than by the door is a thief and a robber. But the sheep will not follow a stranger, only the true shepherd because they know his voice. But they listen to the shepherd and they follow him because they know his voice and they hunger and thirst for righteousness. The multitude who had gathered there were like sheep without a shepherd. He told them that some were not of his fold and did not know his voice and did not follow him. And because they were false shepherds, the sheep knew not their voice and would not follow them. (John 10:1-8)

*And now lest some of you too easily comprehend this parable, I will declare that I am both the door to the Father's sheepfold and at the same time the true shepherd of my Father's flocks. (John 10:6-7) Every shepherd who seeks to enter this fold without me shall fail, and the sheep will not hear his voice. I am the door. Every soul who enters upon the eternal way by the means I have created and ordained shall be saved and will be able to go on to the attainment of the eternal pastures of paradise. (John 10:7,9) But I also am the true shepherd who is willing even to lay down his life for the sheep. The thief breaks into the fold only to steal, and to kill, and to destroy; but I have come that you all may have life and have it more abundantly. He who is a hireling, when danger arises, will flee and allow the sheep to be scattered and destroyed; but the true shepherd will not flee when the wolf comes; he will protect his flock if necessary, lay down his life for his sheep. Verily, verily I say to you, friends and enemies, I am the true shepherd; I know my own and my own know me. I will not flee in the face of danger. I will finish this service of the completion of my Father's will, and I will not forsake the flock which the Father has trusted to my keeping. (John 10:10-15)*

*But I have other sheep which are not of this fold and they shall also hear my voice and then shall you know the voice of one shepherd. (John 10:16)*

Then Jesus went on to tell them that the Father who loves him has put all of his flocks in the domain of his hands for keeping, that he will not desert his sheep and that he would not hesitate to lay down his life in the service of his manifold flocks. But if he laid it down, he would pick it up again as this authority has been given him by the Father. (John 10:17-18)

Now when his followers heard these words they were greatly comforted, while the Pharisees from Jerusalem went into the night saying, *He has either a demon or he is insane.* (John 10:20) Still others said, *He speaks like one having authority; besides who ever saw one having a devil open the eyes of a man born blind and to all of the wonderful things which this man has done?* (John 10:19-21)

Although there were many believers, about half of the Pharisees returned to their homes in Jerusalem the next morning.

Having effectively weeded out the non-believers and the Pharisee hecklers by this sermon on "The Good Shepherd," Jesus was now prepared to give his memorable sermon on "Trust and Spiritual Preparedness" the following afternoon.

By early afternoon, some 3,000 people had gathered to hear Jesus speak along the banks of the Jordan.

After preliminary remarks by Simon Peter, the Master said, *What I have many times said to my apostles and to my disciples I now declare to you: Beware of the leaven of the Pharisees which is hypocrisy, born of prejudice and nurtured in traditional bondage, albeit many of these Pharisees are honest of heart and some of them abide here as my disciples. Presently, all of you shall understand my teaching, for there is nothing now hidden that shall not be revealed to you.* (Luke 12:1-2)

*Very soon, will the things which our enemies now plan in secrecy and in darkness be brought out into the light and be proclaimed from the housetops. And I say to you my friends, when they seek to destroy the Son of Man, be not afraid of them. Fear not those who, although they may be able to kill the body, after that have no more power over you. I admonish you to fear none, in heaven or on earth, but to rejoice in the knowledge of him who has power to deliver you from all unrighteousness and to present you blameless before the judgment seat.* (Luke 12:3-5)

*Are not five sparrows sold for two cents? And yet, when these birds flit about in quest of their sustenance, not one of them exists without the knowledge of the Father, the source of life. To angels the very hairs of your head are numbered. And, if all this is true, why should you live in fear of the many trifles which come upon your daily lives? I say to you: fear not; as you are of much more value than many sparrows.* (Luke 12:6-7)

*And of you who have had the courage to confess faith in my gospel before men, I will presently acknowledge before the angels of heaven; but he who shall knowingly deny the truth of my teachings before men shall be denied by his guardian of destiny even before the angels of heaven.* (Matthew 10:32-33, Luke 12:8-9)

*Say what you will about the Son of Man, and it shall be forgiven you; but he who presumed to blaspheme against God shall hardly find forgiveness.* (Luke 12:10)

*And when our enemies bring you before the rulers of the synagogues and before other high authorities, be not concerned about what you should say and be not anxious as to how you should answer their questions, for the spirit that dwells within you shall certainly teach you in that very hour what you should say in honor of the gospel of the kingdom.* (Luke 12:11-12)

Then Jesus went on to ask the multitudes, how long would they tarry in the valley of decision? And he told them he had come into the world to reveal the Father and to lead them to the Father. The first he had done; the last he would not do without their consent but, he said, *Whosoever will let him, come and freely partake of the water of life.* (Rev. 22:17, Matthew 16:24, Mark 8:34, Luke 9:23, John 3:15-16)

*Day 10:*

# **S**ermon at Gerasa

*(February 18 to February 21, AD 30)*

# Sermon at Gerasa
### 4 Day Period
### February 18 — February 21, AD 30

**Saturday, February 18:** *Jesus is the guest of a wealthy Pharisee at Ragaba. (Luke 11:37) Rebukes the lawyer. (Luke 11:45)*

**Sunday, February 19:** *Apostolic party stops over at Amathus, near the border of Samaria (distance: 5 miles). (Luke 17:11) Encounter the lepers, one of which was a Samaritan — lesson on prejudicial feelings.*

**Monday, February 20:** *Jesus and Apostles enter Gerasa (distance: 14 miles). Met with several influential Pharisees. The way which leads to eternal life is straight and narrow. (Matt. 7:13-14, Luke 13:24) Behold, many who are first will be last and those who are last will be first. (Matt. 20:16, Luke 13:28-30)*

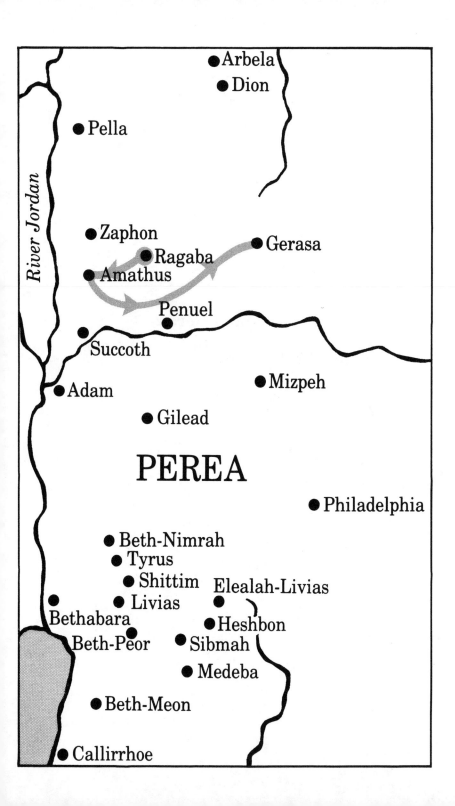

**E**arly February occupied the time of Jesus and the twelve as they journeyed among the cities and villages of northern Perea, before joining with Abner and his associates.

Two days before Jesus and his apostles were to meet up with Abner, they stopped off at the village of Ragaba, where Nathaniel, a wealthy Pharisee, invited them for breakfast. There were about twenty invited guests this Sabbath morning, including a number of fellow Pharisees and several lawyers. Jesus was to be the guest of honor. (Luke 11:37)

The seat to the immediate left of the host was always reserved for the guest of honor, and Jesus took this seat accordingly without first going to the water basin to wash his hands. By now, it was known by a number of Pharisees that Jesus abhorred such ceremonial performances and washed his hands only for the purpose of cleanliness. This supposed defiance of strict

Pharisaic practice upset his host, causing him to raise is eye-brows and whisper to several unfriendly Pharisees seated across from the Master.

Jesus perceived their animosity and arising from his chair told them that he thought that he was invited to this household to break bread as they inquired about his proclamation of the new gospel of the kingdom of God. Instead, he surmised he was there to witness an exhibition of ceremonial devotion to their own self-righteousness. He knew that although some were his friends, the majority of these men were too closed-minded to open their eyes to knowledge and truth.

Speaking to them he said, *How carefully you cleanse the outside of the cups and the platters while the spiritual food vessels are filthy and polluted! You make sure to present a pious and holy appearance to the people, but your inner souls are filled with self-righteousness, covetousness, and all manner of spiritual wickedness.* (Matthew 23:25, Luke 11:39)

And he admonished them that the God of heaven looks at the inner motives of the soul as well as their outer pretenses and their pious profession. And they were told that the giving of alms and the paying of tithes will not spare them from un-righteousness and enable them to stand clean in the presence of God. *Woe upon you Pharisees who have persisted in rejecting the light of life! You are meticulous in tithing and ostentatious in alms giving, but you knowingly spurn the visitation of God and reject the revelation of his love. Woe upon all who shun justice, spurn mercy, and reject truth. Woe upon all those who despise the revelation of the Father while they seek the chief seats in the synagogue and crave flattering salutation in the mar-ketplaces.* (Matthew 23:6, 7, 23; Mark 12:38-39; Luke 11:43)

Jesus was almost ready to depart when one of the lawyers at the table addressed him: *But teacher, when you say this you insult us too. Is there nothing good in the scribes, the Pharisees and the lawyers?* And Jesus replied to this lawyer, *You, like the Pharisees, delight in the first places at the feasts and in wearing long robes while you put heavy burdens, grievous to be borne, on men's shoulders. And when the souls of men stagger under these burdens, you will not so much as lift with one of your fingers. Woe upon you who take the greatest delight in build-ing tombs for the prophets your fathers killed! And that you con-sent to what your fathers did is made manifest when you now plan to kill those who come in this day doing what the prophets did in their day — proclaiming the righteousness of God and revealing the mercy of the heavenly Father. But of all the generations that are past, the blood of the prophets and the apostles shall be required of this perverse and self-righteous generation. Woe upon all of you lawyers who have taken away the key of knowledge from the common people! You yourselves refuse to enter into the way of truth, and at the same time your work hinders all others who seek to enter therein.* (Luke 11:45-52)

And Jesus went on to tell them that they cannot shut the doors of the kingdom of heaven; for they are open to all who have faith to enter. *These portals of mercy shall not be closed by the prejudice and arrogance of false teachers and untrue shepherds who are like whited sepulchers which, while outwardly they appear beautiful, are inwardly full of dead men's bones and all manner of spiritual uncleanliness.* (Matthew 23:13, 27)

When Jesus had finished speaking, he left Nathaniel's table and went out of the house without partaking of food. Although some of these Pharisees were partial to Jesus and actually became his followers, a larger number remained hostile to him, becoming all the more determined to plot and scheme in hopes of catching a few words which could be used to bring him to trial and judgment before the Sanhedrin at Jerusalem. (Luke 11:53-54)

The very next day, Jesus and the twelve headed for Gerasa, stopping over at Amathus, near the border of Samaria. (Luke 17:11) As they approached the city, they encountered a group of ten lepers who stood their distance, but nevertheless called out to the Master to have mercy on them.

Of the ten, nine were Jews and one was a Samaritan. Under normal circumstances, the Jews would have not associated with this Samaritan, but their common affliction overcame any religious prejudice. The apostles, however, still harbored ill feelings toward the Samaritans, as did all Jews.

The enmity between the Jews and the Samaritans had existed for more than half a millennium. Both peoples worshipped the same God; both taught from the same Scriptures and both honored Moses as the first law-giver, but unlike the semitic Jews, the Samaritans had mixed roots which came about in the following manner: After Solomon's death, his kingdom was divided into two regions, Samaria in the north and Judea in the

south. About 700 BC, Sargon, King of Assyria, in subduing a
revolt in central Palestine, carried away into captivity over
25,000 Jews of this northern kingdom of Israel (Samaria) and
replaced them with an equal number of Cuthites, Sepharvites
and the Hamathites, and later still, Aschurbanipal sent other
colonies to Samaria as well.

It was during the period of Babylonian captivity (597-538)
that the Jewish religion of the Old Testament really evolved.
Their hostility towards the Samaritans came about when the
Jewish people returned to their former homeland, and found
the Samaritans were antagonistic to them and worked to prevent the rebuilding of Jerusalem.

Some 200 years later, they assisted the armies of Alexander who reciprocated by allowing the Samaritans to build a
temple on Mount Gerizim. Their priests married heathen women
and worshipped a number of tribal gods, as well as Yahweh.

These Samaritans were spiritually defiled as far as the
Jews were concerned, and from the days of Alexander, they had
no dealings with one another.

Simon Zelotes inherited this prejudice, so when he observed one Samaritan among the Jews, he suggested they pass
the whole group by. But Jesus suggested to Simon that maybe
the Samaritan loved God as much as the Jews and if that were
the case, why sit in judgment of him? Simon was to learn a
lesson that day regarding the gratitude of men and the loving
mercy of God.

Jesus, approaching the lepers, said, *If you would be
made whole, go forthwith and show yourselves to the priests
as required by the law of Moses and they went and they were
made whole. But when the Samaritan saw that he was being
healed, turned back and fell on his knees in front of the Master
praising and glorifying God. While the nine others, the Jews,
were also healed and were grateful for this cleansing, they continued on their way to show themselves to the priests.* (Luke
17:14-16)

As the Samaritan remained kneeling at Jesus' feet, the
Master, looking about, asked, *Were not ten cleansed? Where then
are the other nine, the Jews? Only one, this alien, has returned
to give glory to God* and then he said to the Samaritan, *Arise
and go your way; your faith has made you whole.* (Luke 17:17-19)

It was a difficult lesson for Simon and his brethren not to

allow their prejudicial feelings to rule their hearts. If they were to become efficient ministers of the gospel of the kingdom, they had to first overcome their own personal prejudices, especially towards the Samaritan.

After this brief encounter with the lepers, the apostolic party moved on to the town of Gerasa. Gerasa was a magnificent city marked by a hundred columns of the colonnade that lined the main street; temples, theaters, baths, and an aqueduct all attested to the affluency of this town. Having arrived at Gerasa the next day, Jesus and his apostles met with several influential Pharisees.

These Pharisees had been taught that only the children of Abraham will be saved and only those Gentiles of adoption could ever hope for salvation. They well knew that only Caleb and Joshua, among the hosts that went out of Egypt, lived to enter the promised land. (Numbers 26:65) With this in mind, one of these Pharisees asked Jesus, *Lord, will there be few or many really saved?* (Luke 13:22-23)

And Jesus replied, *The way which leads to eternal life is straight and narrow, that the door which leads thereto is likewise narrow so that those who seek salvation, few can find entrance through this door. You also have a teaching that the way which leads to destruction is broad, that the entrance thereto is wide and that there are many who choose to go this way.* (Matthew 7:13-14, Luke 13:24)

These men were beginning to learn that salvation was a matter of their personal choosing, for Jesus had told them that even if the door to the way of life is narrow, it is wide enough to admit all who sincerely seek to enter, for *I am that door.* And the son will never refuse entrance to any child of the universe who, by faith, seeks to find the Father through the son. (Luke 13:24) But Jesus went on to tell them that there were dangers attached to the postponement of their entrance into the kingdom while they continued to pursue the pleasures of immaturity and indulge in the satisfaction of selfishness. Having refused to enter the kingdom as a spiritual experience, they may subsequently seek entrance thereto when the glory of a better way becomes revealed in the age to come. Said Jesus, *When those who spurned the kingdom when I came in the likeness of humanity seek to find an entrance when it is revealed in the likeness of divinity, then will I say to all such selfish ones: I know not whence you are.* (Luke 13:25-27)

The message was clear. If they rejected the invitation to come when the door of salvation was open, having thus refused to enter by ignoring the son's calling, the door would be shut when they attempted to enter at a later date. This door to salvation would not be open for those who would enter the kingdom for selfish glory; that salvation is not for those who are unwilling to pay the price of wholehearted dedication to doing the Father's will. When the spirit and soul have rejected the Father's kingdom, it is useless in mind and body to stand before this door and knock saying, *Lord open to us; we would also be great in the kingdom.* By then it would be too late, and Jesus would declare to them, *You are not of my fold.*

Looking upon these Pharisees, Jesus continued, *And when you say, 'Did we not eat and drink with you, and did you not teach in our streets?' then shall I again declare that you are spiritual strangers; that we were not fellow servants in the Father's ministry of mercy on earth; that I do not know you.* (Matthew 7:21-23, Luke 13:26-27)

These men well knew the meaning of the verse which states *Depart from me, all you who have taken delight in the works of iniquity.* (Psalm 6:8)

Jesus was offering them assurance that everyone who sincerely desired to find eternal life by entrance into the kingdom of God shall certainly find such everlasting salvation. *But to those of you who refuse this salvation will some day see the prophets of the seed of Abraham sit down with the believers of the Gentile nations in this glorified kingdom to partake of the bread of life and to refresh themselves with the water thereof. And they who shall thus take the kingdom in spiritual power and by the persistent assaults of living faith will come from the north and the south and the east and the west.* (Matthew 8:11)

*And, behold, many who are first will be last, and those who are last will many times be first.* (Matthew 20:16, Mark 10:31, Luke 13:28-30)

It was a difficult message for some of these Pharisees to comprehend. Humility not being their noblest virtue, they had set themselves above the lot. But to others, they were beginning to see that they had to be *born again — born of the spirit — in order to enter the kingdom of God.* (John 3:3-5) And this required them to be honest of heart and sincere in faith, for Jesus told them, *Behold I stand at the doors of men's hearts and knock, and if any man will open to me, I will come in and sup with him, and will feed him with the bread of life.* (Revelation 3:20) And this was the lesson to be learned from Jesus' sermon at Gerasa that, *I am the door, I am the new and living way, and whosoever wills may enter to embark upon the endless truth-search for eternal life.* (John 10:7-9)

*Day 11:*

# **H**ealing in the Philadelphia Synagogue

*(February 22 to February 28, AD 30)*

# Healing in the Philadelphia Synagogue
7 Day Period
February 22-February 28, AD 30

**Wednesday, February 22:** *Jesus, his Apostles and followers arrive at Philadelphia from Gerasa (distance: 22 miles). Jesus heals man with dropsy. (Luke 14:4)*

**Saturday, February 25:** *Jesus heals woman bent in form. (Luke 13:11-13)*

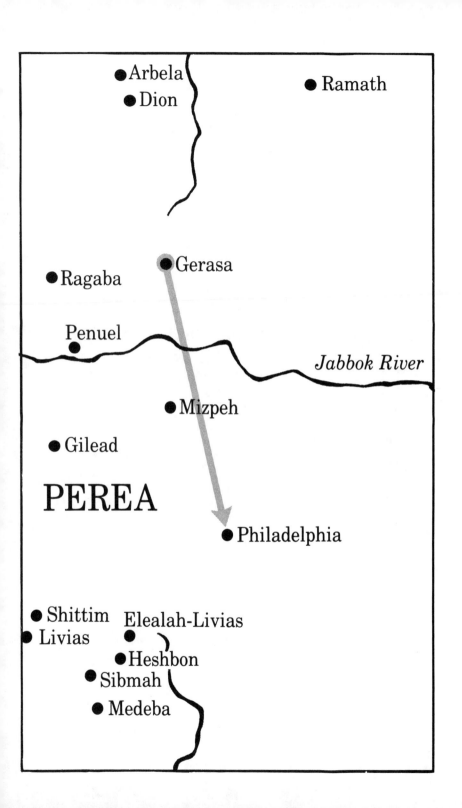

In the first century after Jesus' death, of all the cities in Perea, Philadelphia possessed the largest group of Jews and Gentiles that embraced his teachings. This in the main was primarily due to the efforts of one man — Abner. Until his death in the year AD 74, Abner was to head up the eastern church at Philadelphia. This congregation held more strictly to the religion of Jesus as he lived and taught than any church in its day.

It was because of Abner's uncompromising attitude and his unwillingness to follow Peter and Paul's theology in the early years that so thoroughly isolated his ministry from that of his western brethren.

It was Abner's contention that Paul and his associates partly transferred the issues of eternal life from the individual to the church. Christ thus became the head of the church rather than the elder brother of each individual believer in the Father's family of the kingdom. Paul and his contemporaries applied all of Jesus' spiritual implications regarding himself and the individual believer, to the church as a group of believers, and in doing this, they struck a death-blow to Jesus' concept of the divine kingdom in the heart of the believers.

Nevertheless, for several centuries, this church at Philadelphia was the headquarters of the early Christian church in the south and east, as was Antioch in the north and west. But it was not destined to survive as did the church at Rome and Jerusalem. This schism between Abner's congregation in the east and Peter's and James' (the Lord's brother) in the west continued to widen even after the destruction of Jerusalem in the year AD 70.

Abner could not agree with Peter and James on matters of administration and the jurisdiction of the Jerusalem church. He did not agree with Paul's brand of philosophy and theology, and stubbornly resisted all attempts of Paul to remake the teachings of Jesus so as to present less that was objectionable, first to the Jews, then to the Greco-Roman believers. He even went so far in his later years as to denounce Paul as the "clever corrupter of the life and teachings of Jesus of Nazareth, the son of the living God."

His bitter opposition to Paul's version of Jesus' teachings, coupled with his defiance of James, the Lord's brother, who was supported by Peter, served to isolate his congregation from those in the west who were beginning to evolve a religion about Jesus, as opposed to the religion of Jesus.

It was late Thursday when Jesus and his apostles, along with some 600 followers, arrived in Philadelphia, two days before he was to speak in the synagogue. Abner, who himself had been teaching at the synagogue, arranged for Jesus to teach on the Sabbath. This was accomplished because the synagogue at Philadelphia was not subject to the supervision of the Sanhedrin at Jerusalem and, therefore, had never been closed to Jesus and his associates. This was the first time Jesus would speak in a synagogue since they were closed to him by order of the Sanhedrin.

Because of this fact, and because of his fame as a healer, many Pharisees had come over from Jerusalem and elsewhere to hear him speak.

Now, there lived a wealthy and influential Pharisee, a

follower of Abner, who invited Jesus to his house this Sabbath morning for breakfast. (Luke 14:1)

While Jesus was speaking with Abner at the door, one of the leading Pharisees of Jerusalem entered the room and seated himself in the seat of honor at the left of the host. But since this seat was reserved for the Master, the host beckoned the Pharisee to be seated elsewhere. This dignitary was terribly offended because he was denied the seat of honor.

Towards the end of the meal, there entered from the street a man long afflicted with a chronic disease called dropsy. (Luke 14:2)

Jesus perceived the disdainful look on the Pharisee's face when the man drew near them and sat down upon the floor. Then addressing them he said, *My friends, teachers in Israel and learned lawyers, I would like to ask you a question: Is it lawful to heal the sick and afflicted on the Sabbath day or not?* But knowing Jesus as they did, they all chose to remain silent. Then Jesus went over to the sick man and, taking him by the hand, healed him immediately, telling him to arise and go his way. (Luke 14:4)

Then Jesus turned and, addressing the Pharisees, said, *Which one of you, having a favorite animal that fell in the well on the Sabbath day would not go right out and draw him up?* And again they made no reply. So Jesus began to tell them of a parable on humility. Said Jesus, *My brethren, when you are bidden to a marriage feast, sit not down in the chief seat, lest perchance, a more honored man than you has been invited, and the host will have to come to you and request that you give your place to this other and honored guest. In this event, with shame you will be required to take a lower place at the table. When you are bidden to a feast, it would be the better part of wisdom, on arriving at the festive table, to seek for the lowest place and then take your seat therein, so that, when the host looks over the guests, he may say to you: 'My friend, why sit in the seat of the least? Come up higher; and then you will have honor in the sight of all who are at the table with you.'* (Luke 14:8-10)

And Jesus went on to say, *Forget not, every one who exalts himself shall be humbled, while he who truly humbles himself shall be exalted. Therefore, when you entertain at dinner or give a supper, invite not always your friends, your brethren, your kinsman, or your rich neighbors, that they may in return bid you to their feasts, and thus will you be recompensed. Instead, when you give a banquet, sometimes bid the poor, the maimed and the blind. In this way, you shall be blessed in your heart, for you will know that the lame and the halt cannot repay you for your loving ministry.* (Luke 14:11-14)

When Jesus had finished speaking, one of the lawyers present thoughtlessly said, *Blessed is he who shall eat bread in the kingdom of God* (Luke 14:15) — that being a common saying in those days.

Upon hearing this, Jesus spoke the following parable: *A certain ruler gave a great supper, and having bidden many guests, he dispatched his servants at suppertime to say to those who were invited, 'Come, for everything is now ready.' And they all with one accord began to make excuses. The first said, 'I have just bought a farm, and I need to go look at it; please consider me excused.' And another said, 'I have bought five yoke of oxen, and I must go to receive them, please consider me excused.' And still another said, 'I have just married a wife, and therefore I cannot come.' So the servants went back and reported this to their master. When the master of the house heard this, he was very angry, and turning to his servants, he said, 'I have made ready this marriage feast; the fatlings are killed and all is in readiness for my guests, but they have spurned my invitation; go quickly therefore into the streets and lanes of the city and bring here the poor, the outcast, the blind and the lame that the marriage feast may have guests.' And the servants did as their lord commanded and even then there was room for more guests. Then said the lord to his servants, 'Go now but into the roads and the countryside and constrain those who are there to come in that my house may be filled. I declare that none of those who were first bidden shall taste my supper.' And the servants did as their master commanded, and the house was filled.* (Luke 14:16-24)

Later that Sabbath afternoon, Jesus spoke in the synagogue, which was the first time since they had been closed to him by the Sanhedrin. At the conclusion of the service, Jesus spotted an elderly woman who was much bent in form. He went over to her and touching her bowed-over form said, *Woman, if you would only believe you could be wholly loosed from your spirit infirmity."*And this woman, who for more than 18 years had been bound by fears of depression, believed the words of Jesus, and by faith straightened up immediately. When this woman saw she had been made erect again, she began glorifying

God. (Luke 13:10-13)

Although the congregation at Philadelphia was friendly to Jesus, the chief ruler was not. This official, indignant because Jesus had healed on the Sabbath, stood before the congregation and said, *Are there not six days in which man should do all these works? In these working days come, therefore, and be healed, but not on the Sabbath day.* (Luke 10:14)

After the unfriendly ruler had spoken, Jesus returned to the speaker's platform and said, *Why play the part of hypocrites? Does not everyone of you on the Sabbath, loose his ox from the stall and lead him forth for watering? If such a service is permissible on the Sabbath day, should not this woman, a daughter of Abraham who has been bound down by evil these 18 years, be loosed from this bondage and led forth to partake of the waters of liberty and life, even on this Sabbath day?* And as this woman continued to glorify God, the congregation rejoiced with her, and the ruler was put to shame. (Luke 13:15-17)

Jesus taught again in the synagogue on Sunday, and many of these people were baptized by Abner this day in the river that flowed south of the city.

*Day 12:*

# **E**ncounter at Jericho

*(March 1 to March 6, AD 30)*

# Encounter at Jericho
6 Day Period
March 1 — March 6, AD 30

**Sunday, February 26:** *Jesus informed at Philadelphia that Lazarus was very sick.*

**Wednesday, March 1:** *Jesus departs for Bethany. Tells parable on humility. (Luke 14:8-10) Everyone who exalts himself shall be humbled and he who humbles himself shall be exalted. (Luke 14:11)*

**Wednesday, March 1:** *Jesus arrives in Jericho late afternoon (distance: 28 miles). Tells parable about the good Samaritan. (Luke 10:29-37) The Pharisee sought justice; the publican sought mercy. Taught the law of the universe: Ask and you shall receive; seek and you shall find. (Matt. 7:7-8, Luke 11:9-10)*

**Thursday, March 2:** *Jesus blesses the little children. (Matt. 19:13-15. Mark 10:16, Luke 18:15-17) Enters Bethany (distance: 12 miles), and performs greatest miracle — raising Lazarus from the dead. (John 11:1-44) I am the resurrection and the life. (John 11:25)*

**Monday, March 6:** *Arrive back at Pella camp late evening (distance: 52 miles).*

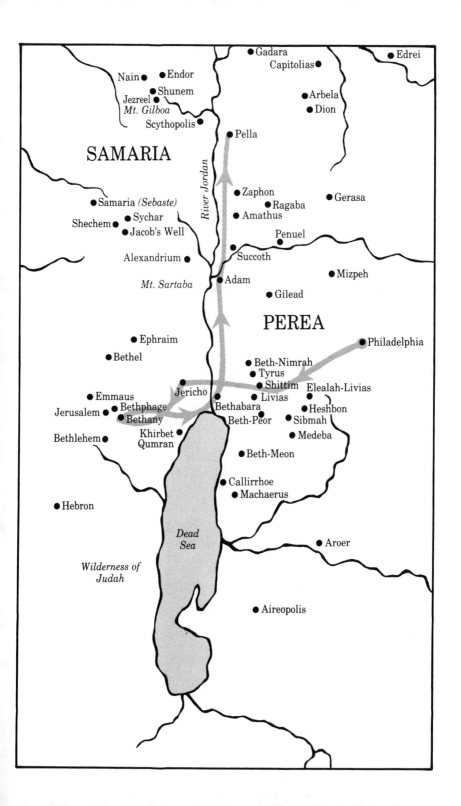

Late Sunday evening, February 26, a runner from Bethany arrived at Philadelphia bringing a message from Lazarus' sisters, Martha and Mary, that he was very sick. This message reached Jesus at the close of the evening conference just about the time he was to retire for the night.

Upon reading the message which said, *Lord, he whom you love is very sick*, Jesus addressed the messenger telling him that *this sickness is really not to the death. Doubt not that it may be used to glorify God and exalt the Son.* (John 11:1-4)

Accordingly, early on Wednesday morning, Jesus said to his apostles, *Let us prepare at once to go into Judea again.*

These apostles knew that the Jewish leaders in Jerusalem were seeking the Master's death and did their best to persuade him not to go. When Jesus would not relent, Thomas addressed his associates saying: *We have told the Master our fears, but he is* determined to go to Bethany. *I am satisfied it means the end; they will surely kill him; but if that is the Master's choice then let us acquit ourselves like men of courage; let us go and die with him.* (Luke 11:16)

And so, on this Wednesday morning Jesus, his apostles and some 50 friends and enemies set out for Bethany in Judea.

About noontime, over lunch, the Master talked to a group of followers on the "Terms of Salvation," ending the lesson with the parable on the Pharisee and the publican (tax collector). (Luke 18:5)

He would tell these men that the Father gives salvation to the children of men, and their salvation is a free gift to all who have the faith to receive sonship in the divine family. There is nothing man can do to earn this salvation. These men would hear again, as Jesus had told the Pharisees so many times before, that works of self-righteousness cannot buy the favor of God, and that much praying in the public will not atone for the lack of living faith in the heart. They could fool men by their outward service, but not God, for he looks into their souls.

Said Jesus, *What I am telling you is well illustrated by two men who went into the temple to pray, the one a Pharisee and the other a publican. The Pharisee stopped and prayed to himself. 'O God, I thank you that I am not like the rest of the men, extortioners, unlearned, unjust, adulterers, or even like this publican. I fast twice a week; I give tithes of all that I get.' But the publican, standing afar off, would not so much as lift his eyes to heaven but smote his breast, saying, 'God, be merciful to me, a sinner.' I tell you that the publican went home with God's approval rather than the Pharisee, for everyone who exalts himself shall be humbled, but he who humbles himself shall be exalted.* (Luke 18:9-14)

Upon arriving early evening in Jericho, Jesus was confronted by a certain lawyer, seeking to entangle him in a compromising situation, knowing both the teachings of Jesus and the law of the prophets. Said the lawyer: *Teacher, I would like to ask you just what I should do to inherit eternal life?* And Jesus replied, *What is written in the law and the prophets: how do you read the Scriptures?* The lawyer answered saying: *To love the Lord God with all your heart, soul, mind and strength, and your neighbor as yourself.* Then said Jesus: *You have answered right, this, if you really do will lead to life everlasting.* (Luke

10:25-28)

Seeking to justify himself while hoping to embarrass Jesus, this crafty lawyer sought to ask the Master another compromising question. Drawing closer to Jesus, he said, *But Teacher, I should like you to tell me just who is my neighbor?* This lawyer knew that the Jewish law defined one's neighbor as "the children of one's people" and hoped to entrap Jesus into making some statement that would contravene the Laws of Moses.

The Jews looked upon all others as "Gentile dogs," although this lawyer knew Jesus felt differently. He therefore hoped to lead the Master into saying something that might contradict their sacred laws.

Jesus, knowing the motives of this insincere man, instead proceeded to tell him and the Jericho audience a story. Said Jesus: *A certain man was going down from Jerusalem to Jericho, and he fell into the hands of cruel brigands, who robbed him, stripped him, and beat him, and departing, left him half dead. Very soon, by chance, a certain priest was going down on that road, and when he saw him, he passed by on the other side. And likewise a Levite also, when he came to the place and saw him, passed on the other side.*

*But a certain Samaritan, who was on a journey, came upon him; and when he saw him he was moved with compassion, and going over to him he bound up his wounds pouring oil and wine on them; and then he put him on his own beast and brought him to an inn and took care of him. And on the next day he took out two denarii and gave them to the innkeeper saying, 'Take care of my friend, and if the expense is more, when I come back, I will repay you.'*

*Now let me ask you: Which of these three turned out to be the neighbor of him who fell among the robbers?*

And when the lawyer realized he had fallen into his own snare, refusing to even mention the word Samaritan, answered, *The one who showed mercy towards him.* (Luke 10:29-37)

But the wisdom of the Master had prevailed upon this crafty and dishonest lawyer, as Jesus merely threw the ball back into his court. He was the one who had to answer the question, "Who is my neighbor?" Had Jesus so answered, it would have directly involved him in the charge of heresy.

This story of the "Good Samaritan" was well received by the people of Jericho and did much to promote brotherly love among all who have subsequently believed the gospel of Jesus.

That same Wednesday evening in Jericho, several un-friendly Pharisees sought to entrap the Master by inducing him to discuss marriage and divorce. (Matthew 19:3, Mark 10:2) But Jesus skillfully avoided their efforts to bring him into conflict with their laws concerning divorce. Though Jesus refused to be drawn into a controversy with these Pharisees concerning di-vorce, he did proclaim a positive teaching of the highest ideals regarding marriage. He exalted marriage as the most ideal and highest of all human relationships.

At this time, the Jerusalem Jews had established lax and unfair divorce practices allowing them to divorce their wives for the most trifling of reasons, such as being a faulty cook or housekeeper or for a better looking woman.

The Pharisees had even gone so far as to teach that divorce in this lax manner was a special dispensation granted the Jewish people, especially the Pharisees. Jesus strongly disapproved of these practices and never sanctioned any divorce practice which gave man any advantage over women; to him marriage was honorable and should be desired by all men.

Under Jewish law, it was not the husband who had to endure the "marital guilt test;" it was the wife. The Old Testa-ment is a grim reminder of the inequities of the marital rights of the sexes under the Laws of Moses. (Numbers 5:12-31) If a man suspected his wife of being untrue to him, he took her to the priest and stated his suspicions. The priest would then pre-pare a concoction consisting of holy water and sweepings from the temple floor. After due ceremony, the accused wife was made to drink this vile potion to the accompaniment of threatening curses. If she was guilty *the water that causes the curse shall enter into her and become bitter, and her belly shall swell, and her thighs shall rot, and the woman shall be accursed among her people.* (Numbers 5:21-22) If by chance she could stomach this dreadful concoction and not show symptoms of physical illness, she was acquitted of the charges made by her jealous husband.

Jesus' mission on earth was exclusively concerned with revelations of spiritual and religious truths and, therefore, he was somewhat reluctant to offer new mandates governing mar-riage and divorce. But when tested by these Pharisees with the question, *Is it lawful for a man to divorce his wife for any cause at all?* Jesus replied, *The Father has directed the creation of male and female and it is the divine will that men and women should find their highest service and consequent joy in the establishment of homes for the reception and training of children, in the creation of whom their parents become co-partners with the makers of heaven and earth. And for this cause, shall a man leave his father and mother and shall cleave to his wife, and they shall become as one.* (Matthew 19:4-5, Mark 10:6-8, Genesis 2:24, Ephesians 5:31)

By evening time, the message regarding marriage and the blessedness of children spread all over Jericho. Consequently, the next morning, scores of mothers and their children came to where Jesus was lodging to have these little ones blessed. When the apostles saw this commotion, they endeavored to turn these women away. But they would have no part of it until the Master had laid hands on their children and blessed them.

Upon hearing his apostles loudly rebuke these mothers, Jesus came out and reproved them for their ill manners, saying *Suffer little children to come to me; forbid them not, for such is the kingdom of heaven. Verily, verily I say to you, whosoever receives not the kingdom of God as a little child shall hardly enter therein to grow up to the full stature of spiritual manhood.* (Mark 10:14-15, Luke 18:16-17)

And when the Master had spoken to his apostles, he received all of the children, laying his hands on them, while he spoke encouraging words of hope to their mothers. (Matthew 19:13-15, Mark 10:14-16, Luke 18:16-17) As a result of these teachings, the status of women was much improved in Palestine.

The very next day, Jesus was to shock all of Palestine by the raising of Lazarus from the dead.

*Day 13:*

# **C**leansing the Temple

*(March 29 to April 3, AD 30)*

# Cleansing the Temple
## 6 Day Period
### March 29 — April 3, AD 30

**Wednesday, March 29:** *Apostolic party rest at Livias. When they kill the Son of Man, be not dismayed, for I declare that on the third day He shall rise. (Matt. 20:17-19, Mark 10:32-34, Luke 1:31-33)*

**Thursday, March 30:** *Jericho (distance: 11 miles) — Jesus restores sight to Bartimaeus, a blind beggar. (Matt. 20:29-34, Mark 10:46-52, Luke 18:35-43) Jesus meets with Zacchaeus, the chief tax gatherer. Today salvation has come to this home. (Luke 19:9)*

**Friday, March 31:** *On the road to Bethany tells a parable about the pounds or minas. (Luke 19:11-27) Arrives at Bethany late afternoon (distance: 12 miles). (John 12:1-2) Stays at the home of Simon. (Mark 14:3) Mary, Lazarus' sister, uses expensive ointment to anoint Jesus' head and feet. (Matt. 26:7-13, Mark 14:3-9, Luke 12:3-8)*

**Sunday, April 2:** *Peter and John procure ass from neighboring village of Bethphage. (Matt. 21:1-3; Mark 11:1-3, Luke 19:28-31) Jesus weeps as he looks upon Jerusalem for the last time. (Luke 19:41) Jesus forecasts the doom of Jerusalem. (Luke 19:43-44) Jesus enters Jerusalem among shouts of praise (distance: 2 miles).*

**Monday, April 3:** *Jesus arrives back in Jerusalem from Bethany and enters temple. Frees the animals and overturns the money tables. (Matt. 21:12-13, Mark 11:15-17, Luke 19:45-46, John 2:14-16) My house shall be called a house of prayer for all nations, but you have made it a den of robbers. Tells parable of the absent landlord. (Matt. 21:33-40, Mark 12:1-9, Luke 20:9-15) Only one sign shall be given you . . . destroy this temple and in three days I will raise it up. (John 2:18-19)*

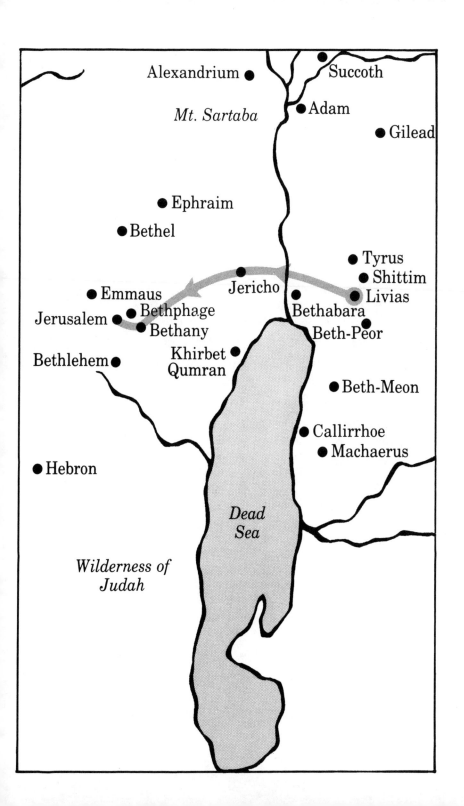

Alexandrium

Succoth

Mt. Sartaba

Adam

Gilead

Ephraim

Bethel

Tyrus

Shittim

Emmaus

Jericho

Livias

Jerusalem

Bethphage

Bethabara

Bethany

Beth-Peor

Bethlehem

Khirbet
Qumran

Beth-Meon

Callirrhoe

Machaerus

Hebron

Dead
Sea

Wilderness of
Judah

I t was the common belief of the Jews regarding the soul of man, that the soul had gone on to the abode of departed spirits before the fourth day had dawned. They allowed that the soul might linger three days, but never into the fourth day.

From the time the runner brought the news of Lazarus' death to Jesus in Philadelphia, to the time he arrived at his tomb in Bethany, it had been well into the fourth day. Several hours had passed since the stone covering the tomb had been rolled into place, and the Master's followers, as well as his enemies, knew there was nothing he could do. So they thought.

Among the several dozen persons standing before the tomb, many were skeptics, and some his bitter enemies. What they witnessed that Thursday afternoon, friend and enemy alike, none would ever forget.

When Jesus directed the stone covering the entrance to the

tomb be rolled away, and when all beheld the prostrate form of Lazarus, wrapped in linen bandages resting on the right lower niche, beginning to rise upon the Master's command, "Come forth," many turned pale from fright and ran in fear. Others were overcome with a sense of awe and astonishment. All were greatly impressed by this manifestation of supernatural power. To some, it was the greatest of miracles, while to others it was the work of the devil.

To the followers of Jesus, this healing of Lazarus represented the greatest manifestation of God's love and compassion — the restoring of a friend's life to a family who truly loved and needed him. To his avowed enemies, this healing was carried out through the power of the prince of devils, and they hastened to Jerusalem to report the incident to the leaders of the Sanhedrin.

By noon the next day, the story of Lazarus' resurrection had spread all over Jerusalem.

That very same afternoon, the Sanhedrin met to deliberate on the question: What should be done with this Jesus of Nazareth? After all, did he not tell those at the tomb that he was *The resurrection and the life*? (John 11:25)

After several hours of debate, a resolution was finally drawn up, proclaiming that he was a menace to all Israel and formally committing the Sanhedrin to a sentence of death, without trial and against all precedent, and this was the first time this body of elders of Israel had gone on record as desiring to decree a death in advance of a trial.

Two weeks following their decree, Jesus and his apostles ministered to the peoples of southern Perea, many of which were Gentiles, while they prepared for the upcoming passover in Jerusalem.

As Jesus and the apostolic party headed towards Jerusalem, the Master knew it would be his last attempt to present his gospel of the kingdom of heaven upon the hearts of men to all who would listen; and he knew that before this Passover week ended, he would take up the cross as the price for human bigotry, religious prejudice and spiritual blindness.

It had been thirty days since the apostles witnessed one of the most amazing events ever to be recorded in the annals of human history — the raising of Lazarus from the dead. In less than a week, they would witness an even more remarkable event.

Resting at Livias, Jesus told the twelve of the fate that awaited him. Said the Master, *The Son of Man will be delivered into the hands of the chief priests and the religious scribes; that they will condemn him and then deliver him into the hands of Gentiles. And they will mock him, scourge him, even spit on him, then condemn him to death. And when they kill the Son of Man, be not dismayed for I declare that on the third day he shall rise.* (Matthew 20:17-19, Mark 10:32-34, Luke 18:31-33)

Although Jesus told his apostles what to expect of him as graphically as he could, these men were still riding an emotional high, having so recently witnessed the extraordinary event of raising Lazarus from the dead. And besides, was not his popularity high with the people, and did he not say to them that he was "the resurrection and the life"?

An air of confidence had consumed these men and this confidence was further enhanced by another miracle Jesus was soon to perform.

As Jesus and the twelve, accompanied by some 200 followers, approached the walls of Jericho, they encountered a throng of beggars, one of which was an elderly man, blind since youth. His name was Bartimaeus, and he well knew of Jesus' power to heal. When he heard the procession passing the city gates, he began to cry aloud, "Jesus, have mercy upon me!" And he continued to cry louder and louder until those near Jesus came over to rebuke him. But this only encouraged him to cry louder.

When Jesus heard the commotion, he told his followers to bring this blind beggar to him. And when his followers complied, Jesus said, *What do you want me to do for you?* And he said, *Lord, I want to receive my sight.* Upon hearing this request and seeing his faith, he said, *You shall receive your sight, go your way; your faith has made you whole.* Immediately, his sight returned and he began following the Master glorifying God and declaring to all how his sight had been restored in Jericho. (Matthew 20:29-34, Mark 10:46-52, Luke 18:35-43)

Later that afternoon, Jesus passed by the customs house of Zacchaeus, the chief publican, a very wealthy man who had heard much about him. Desiring to meet the Master, Zacchaeus tried to press through the crowd; but the crowd was great and he was short, not being able to see over their heads. Realizing he could not penetrate this crowd, and being an enterprising soul, Zacchaeus went on ahead and climbed a sycamore tree whose branches overhung the roadway.

**175**

As Jesus and his apostles passed by, the Master looked up to Zacchaeus and said, *Zacchaeus, hurry and come down for today I must stay at your house.* (Luke 19:5-6)

Now Zacchaeus was bursting with ebullient joy as he hurried back to his home to prepare for Jesus and the twelve.

Approaching his house, the Master and his apostles were confronted by one of the Jericho Pharisees, who, standing nearby, hollered to the crowd that had already gathered, *You see how this man has gone to lodge with a sinner, an apostate son of Abraham, who is an extortioner and a robber of his own people.* (Luke 19:7)

But Jesus only looked upon Zacchaeus with a benign smile. Zacchaeus, wishing to repent in front of Yahweh and country, mounted a stool and spoke to the crowd. *Men of Jericho, hear me! I may be a publican and a sinner but from here on I am going to bestow one-half of all my possessions upon the poor, and if I have defrauded anyone of anything I will give back four times as much.* (Luke 19:8)

When Zacchaeus had finished speaking, Jesus turned to the people and said, *Today salvation has come to this home and you have indeed become a son of Abraham.*

*Marvel not at what I say for I declare that the Son of Man has come to seek and to save that which is lost.* (Luke 19:9-10)

Having spent the evening at the home of Zacchaeus, Jesus and the twelve arose early and departed for the little town of Bethany. Heading down the "road of robbers," they passed the ornate palace of Archelaus, the cruel son of Herod the Great, who possessed all of his father's viciousness and none of his political skill.* Just beyond the palace, along the side of the aqueduct that ran along the road, they paused for lunch.

During lunch, Jesus, surmising the apostles believed he was going to establish the kingdom of God immediately, told them the parable of the pounds or minas. (Luke 19:11-27) In this parable Jesus was telling his followers that, as the king was rejected in his temporal rule, so would the Son of Man be rejected in his spiritual mission. And as the rejected nobleman, Jesus would be calling his twelve special stewards to trade diligently with their trust fund while he was away that they may justify

*Because of the clumsy and brutal manner in which Archelaus dealt with his subjects, he had been removed as the ethnarch of Judea, Samaria and Idumea in the year AD 6.

their stewardship upon his return.

Two miles southeast of Jerusalem lay the small town of Bethany and the smaller hamlet of Bethphage due north. These citizens were all sympathetic to Jesus and his apostles, unlike the cities of Nazareth, Capernaum, and Jerusalem, who had rejected him.

Six days before the Passover, on the evening of the Sabbath, these citizens joined in celebration of the arrival of Jesus at a public banquet held in the home of one Simon, a leading citizen of the village of Bethany. (John 12:1-2)

Among the many guests were the agents of the Sanhedrin, who feared to arrest Jesus in the presence of so many friends. All were in a jovial mood and nothing happened out of the ordinary, until towards the end of the feast, Mary, Lazarus' sister, approached Jesus with a large alabaster cruse of spikenard, a very rare and costly ointment. This precious ointment was equal in cost to the earnings of one man for one year, or in other terms, would provide bread for some 5,000 persons.

Mary loved Jesus and when she heard him forewarn his followers that he must die, she chose to bestow this expensive offering upon the Master while he yet lived.

First anointing the Master's head, she next began on his feet; then taking down her hair, she began to wipe them. The aroma from this perfume permeated the whole house, and everyone was astonished. Although Lazarus, who had so recently been raised from the dead, said nothing when some people began murmuring and showing indignation at the use of such a costly ointment, Judas Iscariot stepped over to where Andrew was reclining and asked why such a costly ointment was not being sold and given to the poor. (John 12:3-5)

Knowing their thoughts, Jesus interceded in Mary's behalf and speaking to those present said, *"Let her alone, everyone of you. Why do you trouble her about this, seeing that she has done a good thing in her heart? To you who murmur and say this ointment should have been sold and given to the poor, the poor you always have with you but you do not always have me. This woman has long saved this ointment for my body at its burial and now she has anointed me beforehand. This woman shall not be reproved for what she has this night done; rather do I say to you that in the ages to come, wherever the gospel shall be preached throughout the whole world, what she has done will be spoken of*

**177**

*in memory of her.* (Matthew 26:7-13, Mark 14:3-9, John 12:3-8)

Having already condemned Jesus to death, when the chief priests heard of this dinner for Jesus and Lazarus they concluded that it would be useless to put the Master to death if they permitted Lazarus to live. Accordingly, they took council and decreed Lazarus' death also. (John 12:10-11)

Meanwhile, Jesus was making his own plans, having decided to make one last public appearance in Jerusalem in conjunction with the Passover.

How to enter the city was the Master's chief concern. His death had already been decreed by the Sanhedrin and his career in the flesh was nearing an end.

Jesus did not wish to make a public entrance into Jerusalem with the pomp and ceremony one might expect of a warrior king who always entered a city upon a horse. Rather he chose to enter as a king on a mission of peace and friendship, who always entered a city riding upon an ass. And Jesus remembered the Scripture in Zachariah (Zachariah 9:9) which said, *Rejoice greatly, O daughter of Zion; shout, O daughter of Jerusalem. Behold, your king comes to you. He is just and he brings salvation. He comes as the lowly one, riding upon an ass, upon a colt, the foal of an ass.* (Matthew 21:4-5, John 12:14-15)

This would be Jesus' manner of entry; no pretension, only placid humility of a man of good will. Accordingly, he directed Peter and John to go to the neighborhood village of Bethphage and procure a colt tied to an ass at the junction of the roads. (Matthew 21:1-3, Mark 11:1-3, Luke 19:28-31)

Having returned with the colt, Jesus mounted the donkey and the procession moved out from Bethany, headed toward the summit of Olivet. A festive crowd of disciples, believers and visiting pilgrims accompanied him on his journey toward Jerusalem.

As they approached the brow of Olivet, one could see the temple towers. This cheerful and joyous crowd beheld the Master weeping as he gazed upon the capital of all Jewry for the last time.

Described by the historian, Pliny, Jerusalem was "by far the most famous city, not only in Judea, but of the whole east." Jerusalem was a proud city, the center of all politics, commerce and religion for all Jewry; a majestic city with cream-colored limestone walls completely surrounding it. Jerusalem's showcase, its temple — the heart of Judaism — built by Herod the Great, was actually the third and largest to occupy the Temple Mount. This Idumean ruler of the Jews, who ruled by Roman decree, desired to ingratiate himself to his subjects by outdoing the fabled Temple of Solomon in both size and opulence.

Solomon's Temple lasted 400 years before it was destroyed by the armies of Babylon. A second temple, built with the support of the Persian King, Cyrus the Great, lasted 500 years. It was destroyed, not by conquering armies, but by Herod himself.

Construction began in the year 20 BC and continued until AD 23. Within two generations of its final stages of construction, both temple and nation would perish at the hands of the Romans.

The entire temple complex covered almost 30 acres. The temple itself was an impressive building with its marble and its colonnades, attracting foreign potentates and other dignitaries who would stand in the Court of Gentiles and gaze in awe-struck wonder upon this magnificent structure.

Herod spared no expense. The walls and the double doors of the two-story sanctuary were covered with gold, topped with golden vines and clusters of golden grapes, "as tall as a man," Josephus would write. Suspended above the golden doors hung an extraordinary tapestry — a panorama of the universe — woven in Babylon.

It is said in the Talmud, "He who has not seen the Temple of Herod, has never seen a beautiful building."

Beyond the temple, where the upper city met the west wall, the three memorial towers of Herod's palace stood out against the green hillside. Not far from Herod's residence stood the regal palace of Caiaphas, surrounded by the homes of the rich.

In spite of the splendor and magnificence of Jerusalem, Jesus knew in his mind the fate of his people if they rejected God's word, and with a tearful voice he was about to tell them of the calamities that would face this city and its people. Looking down upon the vast multitude coming forth from the city to greet him, Jesus said, *O Jerusalem, if you had only known, even you, at least in this your day, the things which belong to your peace, and which you could so freely have had. But now are these glories about to be hid from your eyes. You are about to reject the Son of Peace and turn your backs upon the gospel of salvation. The days will soon come upon you wherein your enemies will cast a trench around about you and lay seize to you on every side; they shall utterly destroy you, insomuch that not one stone shall be left upon another. And all this shall befall you because you knew not the time of your divine visitation.* (Luke 19:41-44)

After speaking to his followers, and as they descended the Mount of Olives, they were met by throngs of high-spirited pilgrims pouring out of the city waving palm branches and shouting hosannas. Accompanying them were many of the Pharisees and his other enemies who greatly feared this vast multitude of believers.

Nearing the city gates, the crowd became more demonstrative, prompting one of the Pharisees walking alongside Jesus to say, *Teacher, you should rebuke your disciples and exhort them to behave more seemly.* And Jesus answered him, *It is only fitting that these children should welcome the Son of Peace, whom the chief priests have rejected. It would be useless to stop them lest in their stead these stones by the roadside cry out.* (Luke 19:39-40) Upon hearing this mild rebuke, the rebuffed Pharisee hastened on ahead of the procession to rejoin his Sanhedrin brethren, reporting to them that *All we do is of no avail as the people have gone mad over him.* (John 12:19)

The city was mightily stirred in ebullient excitement pondering who this man really was, to which his followers replied, *This is the prophet of Galilee, Jesus of Nazareth.* (Matthew 21:10-11)

And this was the air of mixed emotions that pervaded Jerusalem this Passover week — excited anticipation on the part of the multitudes blended with the hostile vengeance of the Jewish leaders.

It had been quite a day for the apostles, as they had never witnessed tens of thousands of people hailing, praising and creating such a commotion over this promised Messiah. They, as a group, were spent to exhaustion.

As the evening approached, this hearty but enervated twelve set down by the treasury, watching the people drop in their contributions, especially the rich, all presumably giving according to the extent of their wealth. In time, there came along a poor widow, scantily attired, and they observed her cast two mites (small coppers) into the trumpet. Upon seeing this, Jesus looked toward his apostles and said, *Heed well what you have just seen. This poor widow cast in more than all the others, for*

*all these others put in out of their surplus some trifle as a gift,*
*but this poor woman, even though she is in want, gave all that*
*she had to live on.* (Mark 12:41-44, Luke 21:1-4)

It was the hypocrisy of the rich Jesus was pointing out;
that they did not really give in accordance with their true
wealth. For this reason, he had not come to the proud and self-
righteous rich, but to the poor and downtrodden — those humble
of spirit.

A tired group of apostles made their way back to Bethany
and the home of Simon that evening. After an early breakfast
in Simon's beautiful garden, Jesus and the twelve set out for what
was to be a very memorable day. About nine o'clock Monday morning, the Master and his apostles arrived at the temple. As Jesus
mounted one of the platforms and began to address the gathering
crowd, his attention was diverted by a drove of some 100 bullocks
which were being driven across the courtyard to a pen. This
commercial trafficking of animals in the temple, coupled with
the commotion from the money changers, was sufficient to stir
the ire of the Master.

Over the years, there grew out of custom the practice of
selling sacrificial animals to the worshippers in the temple
courts. This practice eventually grew into an extensive business
whereby huge profits were made at each of the various feasts.

This custom came about in the following manner: although
it was permissible, according to Scripture (Leviticus 22:18-25),
for a worshipper to provide his own sacrifice, the fact remained
that all animals had to be free from all blemish under Levitical
law, as interpreted by official inspectors of the temple. To dis-
courage such practices, these inspectors were overly strict, and
on numerous occasions the supposedly perfect animal was rejected by the temple examiners to the thorough embarrassment
and humiliation of the worshipper, and so the practice of buying
an animal for sacrifice rather than bringing it became the custom. A portion of these revenues was reserved for the temple
treasury, but the greatest amount went indirectly into the hands
of the ruling high-priestly families.

People were willing to buy these sacrificial animals, even
for an inflated price, because they were assured of not having
to pay additional temple fees.

The other source of revenue in which enormous sums were
made was through the exchange of money. In the times of the

Asmonean dynasty, the Jews coined their own silver money, and it became the practice to regard all temple dues of one-half shekel, as well as all other fees, to be paid with their Jewish coin. The orthodox shekel of Jewish coining became the standard mode of currency in Palestine, creating the need for money changers to be licensed to exchange foreign currencies into Jewish currency.

Everyone visiting the temple, except women, slaves and minors, was required to pay a temple head tax of one-half shekel, a coin about the size of a dime but twice as thick. In Jesus' day, the priests had also exempted themselves from the payment of temple dues.

Since the Jews came to the Passover from all parts of the world ten days before the beginning of Passover, accredited money changers were allowed to erect booths in the principal cities of Palestine for purposes of exchanging foreign currency into Jewish currency to meet the temple dues when reaching Jerusalem. After this ten-day period these money changers moved on to Jerusalem, where they proceeded to reestablish their exchange tables in the courts of the temple. Their service fee was usually a commission of some three to four cents per coin, valued at about ten cents. And for a coin of larger value they were allowed to collect double the smaller coin fee.

In this way, the temple bankers profited not only from the exchange of money for the purchase of sacrificial animals, but also from the payment of vows and the actual selling of the animals.

It was crass commercialism in God's house of worship, in which the temple treasury and the temple rulers profited enormously.

The Jewish pilgrims from foreign provinces strongly resented this method of commerce and profiteering and it was in the midst of this babble of confusion of noisy money changers, merchandisers and cattle sellers that Jesus was to begin his sermon.

The whole scene reeked from exploitation of the devout by a handful of profiteers — God's temple desecrated through the profanation of its rulers.

Jesus, looking about the courtyard, could no longer endure the spiritual abomination that confronted him. Stepping down from the teaching platform in the large courtyard where he so often taught, Jesus spotted a lad driving cattle towards a pen. Taking the whip of cords from the lad's hand, the Master swiftly drove the animals from the temple. Next, he proceeded to open all the gates to every stall, freeing the imprisoned animals.

Never had these pilgrims witnessed such a positive show of defiance against these long-time profiteers. They were electrified. And when Jesus began to overturn the tables of the money changers, they shouted their approval, participating themselves in this act of "cleansing the temple."

By the time the nearby Roman guards had appeared on the scene, the crowds had regained their composure and Jesus was again on the speaker's stand addressing them. Said the Master, *You have this day witnessed that which is written in the Scriptures: 'My house shall be called a house of prayer for all nations, but you have made it a den of robbers.'* (Matthew 21:12-13, Mark 11:15-17, Luke 19:45-46, John 2:14-16)

Before he could continue, this enthusiastic assembly broke out in hosannas of praise that the commercial interest and profiteers had been ejected from the temple. (Matthew 21:15)

By this time, several priests had arrived on the scene and one of them spoke to the Master saying: *Do you not hear what the Levites say?* And the Master replied, *Have you never read, out of the mouths of babes and sucklings has praise been perfected?* (Psalm 8:2, Matthew 21:16)

The greatest obstacle in the spiritual path to God is man's own intellect. When the intellectual pride in self-accomplishment overshadows personal humility, the ego grows. And when the human ego so dominates the mortal mind, it obscures any recognition of the Father's spirit within.

Jesus well knew the intellectual pride of his adversaries and to appeal to the leadings of their hearts was well-nigh impossible. They were dumbfounded at his remarks, and became all the more hardened and determined in setting about to destroy him. (Mark 11:18, Luke 19:47)

Their spiritual circuits were all but severed for the majority of these men, as the door at which the Son of God stood was about to close on them forever. These men subscribed to the letter of the law — the intellectual content of religion — and were subject to the bondage of traditional dogmatism. Their theology had mastered their religion, allowing it to become a doctrine instead of a life. They just could not grasp the faith aspects of the Master's teachings. Faith — human religious insight — comes from revelation and can be elevated only by personal mortal experience with the spirit of God that resides in man. But for these members of the Sanhedrin, their intellects would rule the day and, accordingly, at their noon session it was unanimously agreed by those in attendance that Jesus must be speedily destroyed.

It was early afternoon when a group of these elders of Israel approached Jesus asking the question: *By what authority do you do these things? Who gave you this authority?* (Matthew 21:23, Mark 11:27-28, Luke 20:1-2) Authority was the "watchword" of all Jewry and these leaders well knew that official authority had to come from the Sanhedrin. Only the Sanhedrin could ordain an elder or teacher, and such a ceremony had to take place in the presence of at least three persons who had previously been ordained. After completing the ceremony, the title of "rabbi" was conferred upon the individual, allowing him to teach the law, as well as to act as a judge, in matters brought to him for adjudication. Lack of this "Sanhedrin bestowed authority" in pretentious public teaching was looked upon as indicating either "ignorant presumption or open rebellion."

Therefore, the rulers had come upon Jesus to directly challenge his licensed authority to teach in hopes of discrediting him in front of his followers.

Knowing their motives, Jesus countered their question with one of his own. Said the Master, *I would also like to ask you one question, which if you will answer me, I likewise will tell you by what authority I do these works. The baptism of John, whence was it? Did John get his authority from heaven or from men?* (Matthew 21:24-25, Mark 11:29-30, Luke 20:3-4)

Once again, Jesus had devised a two-edged sword in which to combat their verbal assault. After withdrawing for a moment to ponder the question among themselves, his antagonists soon found the ball was back in their court. They were the ones backed into a corner and somehow had to skillfully maneuver out of it to save face.

They reasoned that if they chose to say from heaven, then will he say, why did you not believe him, and then might add that he received his authority from John. On the other hand, if they said from men, then the multitude might turn upon them, for most of the people held that John was a prophet, and so they were compelled to confess before Jesus and the people that as the religious teachers of Israel they could not express an opinion on John's mission. And when they had spoken, Jesus, looking down upon them said, *Neither will I tell you by what authority I do these things.* (Matthew 21:25-27, Mark 11:31-33, Luke 20:5-8)

Unable to tactfully extricate themselves from their own entrapment, these elders of the Sanhedrin withdrew for the day. But the people were not slow to discern the dishonesty and insincerity of these questions by these Sanhedrin leaders.

The "cleansing of the temple" earlier that day exposed the corrupt practices of base men, profiteering at the expense of the poor and the unlearned. Now the multitudes were beginning to discern the self-serving motives and designing hypocrisy of Jesus' enemies.

To those Pharisees that still remained, Jesus looked down upon them and said, *Since you are in doubt about John's mission and arrayed in enmity against the teaching and the work of the Son of Man, give ear while I tell you a parable: A certain great and respected landholder had two sons, and desiring the help of his sons in the management of his estates, he came to one of them saying, 'Son, go to work today in my vineyard' and he answered and said, 'I will sir' and he did not go. And he came to the second son and said the same thing. But he answered and said, 'I will not,' yet he afterward regretted it and went. Which of the two did his father's will?* And they all said, *The latter* and then said Jesus: *Truly I say to you that the publicans and harlots, even though they appear to refuse the call to repentance, shall see the error of their way and go into the kingdom of God before you.* (Matthew 21:28-31)

Jesus' enemies scoffed at these words, but the people could distinguish between these Sanhedrin leader's pretensions of serving the Father in heaven while literally refusing to do the work of the Father. They could teach, but they would not be taught. And when it came to teaching, Jesus would tell them, *It was not you the Pharisees and scribes, who believed John, but rather the publicans and sinners; neither do you believe my teaching, but the common people hear my words gladly.* (Matthew 21:31-32)

When Jesus finished, the chief Pharisees and the scribes withdrew for council among themselves. This interlude gave the

Master an opportunity to again address the multitude, and turning to them, he told the parable of the absent landlord. Said Jesus, *There was a good man who was a householder, and he planted a vineyard. He set a hedge about it, dug a pit for the wine press, and built a watchtower for the guards. Then he let his vineyard out to tenants while he went on a journey. And when the harvest time grew near he sent his servants to receive his rental. But the wine growers refused to give these servants the fruits due their master; instead they fell upon the servants, beating one, killing another and stoning a third. Again, the householder sent another group of more trusted servants to the tenants, and they were treated in the same manner. Then the householder sent his favorite servant, his steward, and him they killed. And still in patience and forbearance the owner said, 'They may mistreat my servants but surely they will show respect for my beloved son.' But when the wicked tenants saw the son, they reasoned among themselves saying, 'This is the heir, let us kill him that the inheritance may be ours.' So they laid hold on him, and after casting him out of the vineyard, they killed him. When the lord of the vineyard shall hear how they have rejected and killed his son, what will he do to those ungrateful and wicked servants?* (Matthew 21:33-40, Mark 12:1-9, Luke 20:9-15)

When the people heard this parable, they perceived correctly that it was referring to the Jewish nation and its treatment of the prophets and the impending rejection of Jesus and the gospel of the kingdom.

And they answered: *He will destroy those miserable men and let out his vineyard to other vinegrowers who will pay him the proceeds at the proper season.* (Matthew 21:41, Mark 12:9, Luke 20:16) And when they recognized their own plight, they said to one another, *May it never be.* (Luke 20:16)

About this time, a group of Sadducees and Pharisees were making their way through the crowd, and as they edged their way toward Jesus and drew near to him, he said, *You know how your fathers rejected the prophets and you well know that you are set in your hearts to reject the Son of Man. Did you never read in the Scripture about the stone which the builders rejected, and which, when the people had discovered it, was made into a corner stone?* (Psalm 118:22) *And so once more I warn you that, if you continue to reject this gospel, presently will the kingdom of God be taken away from you and.be given to a people willing*

*to receive the good news and to bring forth the fruits of the spirit.
And there is the mystery about the stone, seeing that who so falls
upon it, while he is thereby broken in pieces, shall be saved; but
on whomsoever this stone falls, he will be ground to dust and
his ashes scattered to the fourwinds.* (Matthew 21:42-44, Mark
12:10, Luke 20:16-18)

When the Jewish leaders heard these words, they surmised
Jesus was referring to them, and they greatly desired to lay
their hands on him, but feared the multitude. Again, they withdrew in anger to hold further counsel among themselves on how
to bring about the Master's death. That evening, both the Sadducees and the Pharisees collaborated on how best to entrap
Jesus the next day. (Matthew 21:45-46, Mark 12:12, Luke 20:19)

These Jewish leaders were exasperated, frustrated and
angered, much like a trapped hornet that persistently attacks
a closed window to the point of exhaustion, never coming to
realize there is a small crack in the door in which to free itself.
Eventually it is consumed by total exhaustion and dies, never
finding its path to freedom, as the light it pursued was too
blinding for it to see and search for anything else.

Much like the hornet who chose to follow a deceiving light,
these Sanhedrin leaders were spiritually blinded by their own
strict adherence to their codes of law, and when the door of
living truth was opened to them, they, like the hornet, could
not find it, for they were inextricably bound to their olden religion of ceremony, tradition and authority.

And much like the doomed hornet, their narrow-minded-
ness, pride, anger and hostility would consume their thoughts
which governed their actions, making it well-nigh impossible
to seek the narrow path of righteousness, love, compassion and
service — the path to freedom.

Rejecting the Master's gospel of living truth, they chose
to remain in the pond of stagnation; it was only a matter of
time, in accordance with natural laws of cause and effect (Galatians 6:7), that they would be consumed, taking their people
with them.

After these Sanhedrin leaders had withdrawn, Jesus once
again addressed the people on the parable of the wedding feast.
(Matthew 22:1-13) Upon the conclusion of this parable concerning a thoughtless people who made light of the calling of their
king, Jesus was about to step down from the speaker's platform

when a sympathetic believer stepped forward and asked, *But Master, how shall we know about these things? How shall we know that you are the Son of God?* And Jesus replied, *Only one sign shall be given you.* And Jesus, then pointing to his own body, said, *Destroy this temple, and in three days I will raise it up.* (John 2:18-19)

But the people did not understand him and talking among themselves said, *It took forty-six years to build this temple and he says he will destroy it and raise it up in three days.* But Jesus was speaking to the temple of his body. Even his own apostles did not comprehend the significance of this statement, but subsequently, after his resurrection, they recalled what he had said. (John 2:20-22)

It had been a long day for the Master and his apostles, a day of teaching intermingled with numerous interruptions and disruptive clashes with the Jewish leaders.

There was little more he could give in the way of meaningful instruction that memorable Monday and, as it was approaching late afternoon, Jesus beckoned to his apostles that he desired to leave the temple and go to Bethany for the evening meal and a night of rest.

# Day 14:

# **L**ast Temple Discourse

*(April 4, AD 30)*

# Last Temple Discourse
## April 4, AD 30
## Teaching of This Day

**To the students:** *Render to Caesar the things that are Caesar's and render to God the things that are God's. (Matthew 22:21)*

**To the lawyer:** *On these two commandments hang all the law and the prophets: you shall love the Lord, your God, with all your heart and with all your soul, with all your mind and all your strength. And you shall love your neighbor as yourself. (Matthew 22:37-39, Mark 12:30-31, Luke 10:27)*

**To the Greeks:** *While you have the light, believe in the light that you may become sons of the light. (John 12:35-36)*

**To the temple audience:** *He who would be the greatest among you, should become the server of all. (Mark 10:43-44)*

**To his Apostles:** *A new commandment I give you, that you love one another even as I have loved you, that you also love one another. (John 13:34)*

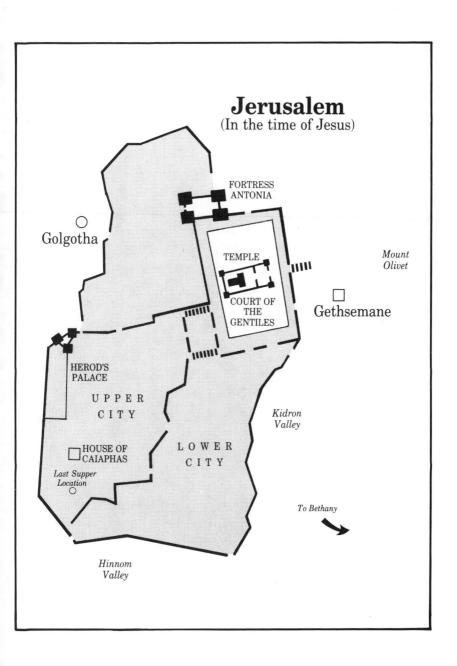

# Jerusalem
## (In the time of Jesus)

FORTRESS
ANTONIA

Golgotha

TEMPLE

Mount
Olivet

COURT OF
THE
GENTILES

Gethsemane

HEROD'S
PALACE

UPPER
CITY

Kidron
Valley

HOUSE OF
CAIAPHAS

LOWER
CITY

Last Supper
Location

To Bethany

Hinnom
Valley

**J**esus was now in the last week of his mortal existence on the planet. Nevertheless, he would attempt one last time to persuade the Pharisees that even they must submit to God's will for their personal salvation.

Earlier this Tuesday morning, Jesus and his apostles pitched their tents in the hillside ravine overlooking the public camping park at Gethsemane, on a plot of ground belonging to Simon of Bethany.

At the home of Simon, not far from camp, Jesus met with some of his followers and the women's corps. At this meeting, he bid farewell to Lazarus, instructing him to flee to Philadelphia in Perea, where he would be safe in the tetrarchy of Philip.

After talking with each of the apostles, he departed from Jerusalem with Andrew, Peter, James and John, while the others left for the Gethsemane camp.

On the prior evening, a council had been held between the

Sanhedrin and some fifty additional leaders, comprised of Pharisees and Sadducees. It was the concensus of these men that Jesus should not be arrested in public because of his great popularity with the common people. They also agreed that Jesus should be discredited in public before being brought to trial. Accordingly, that evening, these men devised a number of questions that were designed to entrap the Master and to embarrass him before the people. (Matthew 22:15, Mark 12:15, Luke 20:20)

When Jesus arrived at the temple the following morning, he had hardly begun to teach when a group of young students, who had been rehearsed for this purpose, confronted the Master with a question designed to entrap him no matter how he answered. Said their leader, *Master, we know you are a righteous teacher, and we know that you proclaim the ways of truth, and that you serve only God, for you fear no man and that you are no respecter of persons. We are only students, and we would know the truth about a matter which troubles us; our difficulty is this: Is it lawful for us to give tribute to Caesar? Shall we give or shall we not give?* Jesus, perceiving their hypocrisy and craftiness replied, *Why do you then come to tempt me? Show me the tribute money and I will answer you.* And when they handed him a denarius, he examined it and said, *Whose image and superscription does this coin bear?* And they answered, Caesar's. Then Jesus said, *Render to Caesar the things that are Caesar's and render to God the things that are God's.* (Matthew 22:16-21, Mark 12:14-17)

This question was designed to be a two-edged sword, for if Jesus would dare to advise against the payment of tribute to Caesar, the Jewish leaders would go at once before the Roman authorities and charge him with sedition. On the other hand, if he should advise the payment of tribute to Caesar, such a pronouncement would greatly wound the national pride of his Jewish followers and turn them away from him.

To the chagrin of these young scribes, Jesus skillfully avoided their trap by answering in such a way as to employ his own two-edged sword — a double reply.

To have answered no to their question would have been equivalent to inciting rebellion; to have answered yes would have shocked the deep-rooted nationalist sentiments of that day.

And these youths, who so eagerly sought to entrap him, marveled at the unexpected sagacity of the Master's answer.

(Matthew 22:22, Mark 12:17, Luke 20:26)

Jesus was about to start his teaching when a group of Sadducees approached him. These learned but crafty men had devised another question in which they hoped to entrap him. Said their leader, *Master, Moses said that if a married man should die, leaving no children, his brother should take the wife, and raise up seed for the deceased brother. Now there occurred a case where a certain man who had six brothers died childless. His next brother took his wife but also soon died, leaving no children. Likewise did the second brother take the wife, but he also died leaving no offspring. And so on until all six of the brothers had had her and all six of them passed on without leaving children. And then after them all, the woman died herself. Now, what we would like to ask you is this: In the resurrection, whose wife will she be since all these brothers had her?* (Matthew 22:23-28, Mark 12:18-23, Luke 20:27-33)

These Sadducees were hoping to catch Jesus on some technicality as to possibly referring to the prophets in his answer to them, as this religio-political sect only acknowledged the five so-called books of Moses, and not the teachings of the prophets, as the foundation of their doctrinal dogmas. Hoping Jesus would take their bait, they could then ridicule him in public so as to discredit his reputation with the people.

Once again, Jesus met their challenge head on by answering this insincere question in a forthright and direct manner. Said the Master, *You all do err in asking such questions because you know neither the Scriptures nor the living power of God. You know that sons of this world can marry and are given in marriage, but you do not seem to understand that they who are accounted worthy to attain the worlds to come, through the resurrection of the righteous neither marry nor are given in marriage. Those who experience the resurrection from the dead are more like the angels of heaven, and they never die. These resurrected ones are eternally the Sons of God; pursuing life eternal. Even Moses understood this for in connection with his experiences at the burning bush, he heard the Father say, 'I am the God of Abraham, the God of Isaac, and the God of Jacob.'* (Matthew 22:29-32, Mark 12:23-27, Luke 20:34-38)

Once again his enemies marveled at the wisdom of his answer and as the Sadducees withdrew, some of the Pharisees so forgot themselves as to exclaim, *True, true, Master, you have well answered these unbelieving Sadducees.* The Sadducees dared not ask him any more questions. (Matthew 22:33, Luke 20:39-40)

The Pharisees, realizing that the shoe was on the other foot in that it was the Sadducees who were discredited, amused themselves at their obvious discomfiture.

It was now the Pharisees' turn to engage the Master in an attempt to discredit him. Accordingly, they sent forth one of their own, a lawyer who addressed Jesus: *Master, I am a lawyer and I would like to ask you which, in your opinion, is the greatest commandment?* and Jesus answered, *There is but one commandment, and that one is the greatest of all, and that commandment is: 'Hear O Israel, the Lord our God, the Lord is one; and you shall love the Lord your God with all your heart and with all your soul, with all your mind and with all your strength.' This is the first and great commandment. And the second is: 'You shall love your neighbor as yourself.' There is no other commandment greater than these; on these two commandments hang all the law and the prophets.* (Matthew 22:35-40; Mark 12:28-31; Luke 10:25-27)

The lawyer, perceiving Jesus to have answered in accordance with the highest concepts of the Jewish religion and not being able to find fault in his answer replied: *Of a truth Master, you have well said that God is one and there is none beside him; and that to love him with all the heart, understanding and strength, and also to love one's neighbor as oneself, is the first and great commandment, and we are agreed that this great commandment is much more to be regarded than all the burnt offerings.* And when Jesus saw that he had answered intelligently, he looked down upon him and said, *My friend, I perceive that you are not far from the kingdom of heaven.* (Luke 12:32-34)

Now there were several other groups of scribes and Pharisees in attendance, all prepared to engage Jesus with mischievous questions designed to ensnare him, but alarmed by the discomfiture of their associates, they dared not ask him anymore questions in public. (Mark 12:34)

Since it was approaching noon hour, Jesus chose not to continue his teaching and since no more questions were forthcoming, he chose to ask the Pharisees one. Said Jesus: *Since you ask me no more questions, I would like to ask you one. What do you think of the Deliverer? That is, whose son is he?* After a brief pause, one of his scribes answered, *The Messiah is the son of David.* And since Jesus knew that there had been much debate, even among his disciples, as to whether or not he was the son of David, he asked this further question: *If the Deliverer is indeed the son of David, how is it that in the Psalms which you accredit to David, he himself, speaking in the spirit, says, 'The Lord said to my Lord, sit on my right hand until I make your enemies the footstool of your feet.' If David calls him Lord, how then can he be his son?* (Matthew 22:41-46, Mark 12:35-37, Luke 20:41-44) (Psalm 110:1)

A dead silence pervaded this congregation as none of the scribes and chief priests made an attempt to answer him. They all thought it the better part of valor not to engage the Master in any further discussion.

It was not until after the Master's death that these rulers attempted to change the interpretation of this Psalm, so as to make it refer to Abraham instead of the Messiah. Still others sought to change the authorship of this Psalm from that of David.

A short time earlier, the Sadducees had suffered embarrassment; now they were delighted by the Pharisees discomfiture. This whole encounter with Jesus at the temple backfired on these antagonists, and in spite of their efforts to entrap him, they were the ones who suffered embarrassment and humiliation. But throughout this whole confrontation, the people marveled at the Master's wisdom and received him gladly. (Mark 12:37)

About the same time the Master was departing from the temple, Philip, who did not attend the discussion, was approached by a group of believing Greeks from Alexandria, Athens and Rome, seeking to speak with Jesus. (John 12:20-22)

Philip had been on his way to the marketplace seeking supplies for the new camp near Gethsemane. Somewhat surprised at this sudden encounter with these foreign Gentiles, Philip had them wait where they were while he set out to locate the Master. Now knowing the whereabouts of Jesus, he headed for the home of Joseph where the other apostles had gathered for lunch. After talking the matter over with Andrew, the two of them returned to the waiting Greeks, where upon all of them set out for the home of Joseph.

By the time they had arrived, Jesus was waiting to receive them.

Much of this discussion centered around the rejection of the Son of God by the children of Abraham and, in doing so, they were rejecting the Father; for he had performed many signs before them, yet they were not believing him. *But truly did the Prophet Isaiah refer to the people when he wrote: 'Lord, who has believed our teaching? And to whom has the Lord been revealed?'* (Isaiah 53:1)

*Truly have the leaders of my people deliberately blinded their eyes that they see not, and hardened their hearts lest they believe and be saved. All these years have I sought to heal them of their unbelief that they may be recipients of the Father's eternal salvation. I have come as a light into the world that everyone who believes in me may not remain in darkness. I know that not all of you have failed me; some of you have indeed believed in my message. But because of the Pharisees you shrink from open confession of the truth lest they cast you out of the synagogue. Some of you are tempted to love the glory of men more than the glory of God. But I say to you, he who beholds me beholds the one who sent me.* (John 12:37-46)

*If my fellow countrymen, the Jews, choose to reject me and to refuse my teachings, I will not sit in judgment on them, for I come not to judge the world but to offer it salvation. Nevertheless, they who reject me and refuse to receive my teaching shall be brought to judgment in due season by my Father and those whom he has appointed to sit in judgment on those that reject the gift of mercy and the truths of salvation. Remember, all of you, that I speak not of myself, but that I have faithfully declared to you that which the father commanded I should reveal to the children of men, and these words which the Father directed me to speak to the world are words of divine truth, everlasting mercy, and eternal life.* (John 12:44-50)

*But to both Jew and Gentile I declare the hour has come when the son of Man will be glorified. You well know that except a grain of wheat falls into the earth and dies, it abides alone; but if it dies in good soil, it springs up again to life and bears much fruit. He who selfishly lives his life stands in danger of losing it but he who is willing to lay down his life for my sake and the gospel's shall enjoy a more abundant existence on earth and in heaven, life eternal. If you will truly follow me, even after I have gone to the Father, then shall you become my disciples and the sincere servants of your fellow mortals.* (Matthew 10:39,

16:25; Mark 8:35, 9:24; Luke 17:33; John 12:23-26)

*I know my hour is approaching, and I am troubled. I perceive that my people are determined to spurn the kingdom; my heart aches for my people, and my soul is distraught by that which lies just before me. What shall I say as I look ahead and discern what is about to befall me? Shall I say, 'Father, save me from this awful hour?' No! For this very purpose have I come into the world and even to this hour. Rather will I say, and pray that you will join me: Father, glorify your name; your will be done.* And when Jesus had thus spoken, there came a voice from heaven saying, *I have both glorified it and will continue to glorify it.* And when the multitude heard this, they all said to one another, *An angel has spoken to him.* (John 12:27-29)

Then Jesus continued to speak, *All this has not happened for my sake but for yours. I know of a certainty that the Father will receive me and accept my mission on your behalf, but it is needful that you be encouraged and be made ready for this fiery trial which is just ahead.* (John 12:30-31)

And Jesus went on to tell these men that victory would eventually crown their efforts to enlighten the world and liberate mankind; that the old order was bringing itself to judgment and all men would become free by the light of the new spirit which he would soon pour out upon all flesh, after he ascended into heaven.

*And now I declare to you that I, if I be lifted up from the earth, will draw all men to myself and into fellowship with my Father. You have believed that the Deliverer would abide on earth forever, but I declare that the Son of Man will be rejected by men, and that he will go back to the Father.* (John 12:32-34)

*Only a little time with the living light be among this darkened generation. Walk while you have this light so that the oncoming darkness and confusion may not overtake you. He who walks in the darkness knows not where he goes; while you have the light believe in the light in order that you may become sons of the light.* (John 12:35-36)

And then Jesus bid them all to return to the temple where he would speak his farewell words to the chief priests, the scribes, the Pharisees, the Sadducees, the Herodians and the benighted rulers of Israel.

Not much was said as this somber entourage headed through the narrow streets of Jerusalem toward the temple.

It was shortly after two o'clock this Tuesday afternoon when Jesus, accompanied by eleven of the apostles, Joseph of Arimathia, thirty or so Greeks and a number of other disciples arrived at the temple for what was to be his last discourse to the Jewish leaders and his avowed enemies.

On this afternoon the temple was unusually quiet and orderly as the money-changers had not dared to return since Jesus had driven them out the previous day.

Before beginning the discourse, Jesus looked benignly upon his audience, telling them of the long time he had been with them going up and down the land proclaiming the Father's love for the children of men. He said that they had seen the light and, by faith, had entered the kingdom of heaven; that many sick and afflicted had been made whole because they believed. But to the Pharisees he said, *All of my proclamation of truth and healing of disease has not opened the eyes of those who refuse to see light. There are those who are determined to reject this gospel of the kingdom.* (Matthew 8:2-3, Mark 1:40-43, Luke 5:12-13)

And this congregation was further told by Jesus that in every manner consistent with doing his Father's will, he and his apostles had done their utmost to live in peace while conforming with the reasonable requirement of the Laws of Moses and the traditions of Israel. Even though the Master and his apostles persistently sought peace, the leaders of Israel would not have it. By rejecting the truth of God and the light of heaven, they were aligning themselves on the side of error and darkness. There cannot be peace between light and darkness, between life and death, between truth and error they were told.

In some ways, this discourse was an eleventh-hour plea for those spiritually blinded teachers and hypocritical leaders to turn from the ways of man to the ways of God, and accept his mercy. Jesus was giving them one last chance to receive the word of heaven and to welcome the Son of Man.

Although there were many believers in the audience, the majority of the Jewish rulers were antagonistic to Jesus' teachings. These men were about to hear that if they continued to reject this revelation of God to man, the kingdom of heaven would be given to other peoples, to those who will receive it with joy and gladness; that these leaders were about to lose their positions in the world as the standard-bearers of eternal truth and the custodians of the divine law.

Jesus, speaking to his audience, said, *In all these matters do whatsoever they bid you and observe the essentials of the law but do not pattern after their evil works. Remember this is the sin of these rulers: they say that which is good, but they do it not.* (Matthew 23:2-3)

*You well know how these leaders bind heavy burdens on your shoulders, burdens grievous to bear and that they will not lift as much as one finger to help you bear these weighty problems. They have oppressed you with ceremonies and enslaved you by traditions.* (Matthew 23:4, Luke 11:46)

And Jesus had more denunciation for these false teachers and bigoted rulers.

*Furthermore, these self-centered rulers delight in doing their good works so they will be seen by men. They make broad their phylacteries and enlarge the borders of their official robes. They crave the chief places at the feasts and demand the chief seats at the synagogues. They covet laudatory salutations in the marketplaces and desire to be called rabbi by all men. And even while they seek all this honor from men they secretly lay hold of widow's houses and take profit from the services of the sacred temple. For a pretense these hypocrites make long prayers in public and give alms to attract the notice of their fellows.* (Matthew 23:5-7; Mark 12:38-40; Luke 20:46-47, 11:43)

And Jesus had still more to say on the subject of exalting oneself over that of his fellows.

*Remember, I have taught you that he who would be greatest among you should become the server of all.* (Mark 10:43-44) In essence he said, *If you presume to exalt yourselves before God, you will certainly be humbled; but who so truly humbles himself will surely be exalted. Seek in your daily lives, not for self-glorification, but the glory of God. Intelligently subordinate your own wills to the will of the Father in heaven.* (Mark 9:35, 43-44)

Jesus, in addressing the Jewish rulers, was telling them that all men must play down their own self-importance, that to exalt themselves over their fellow man for personal aggrandizement does not gain them favor with the Father, for the Father is no respecter of persons.

Said Jesus, *Woe upon you, scribes and Pharisees, hypocrites! You would shut the doors of the kingdom of heaven against sincere men because they happen to be unlearned in the ways of your teaching. You refuse to enter the kingdom and at the same time do everything within your power to prevent all others from entering. You stand with your backs to the doors of salvation and fight with all who would enter therein.* (Matthew 23:13)

*Woe upon you, scribes and Pharisees, hypocrites that you are! For you do indeed encompass land and sea to make one proselyte, and when you have succeeded you are not content until you have made him twofold worse than he was as a child of the heathen.* (Matthew 23:15)

*Woe to you, scribes and Pharisees, hypocrites, because you devour widow's houses and demand heavy dues of those who would serve God as they think Moses ordained! You who refuse to show mercy, how can you hope for mercy in the worlds to come?* (Matthew 23:14)

*Woe upon you, false teachers, blind guides. What can be expected of a nation when the blind lead the blind? They both shall stumble into the pit of destruction.* (Matthew 23:16, Mark 15:14, Luke 6:39)

*Woe upon you who dissimulate when you take an oath! You are tricksters since you teach that a man may swear by the temple and break his oath, but whosoever swears by the gold in the temple must remain bound. You are all fools and blind. You are not even consistent in your dishonesty, for which is the greater, the gold or the temple which has supposedly sanctified the gold? You also teach that if a man swears by the altar, it is nothing; but that if one swears by the gift that is upon the altar, then shall he be held as a debtor. Again, are you blind to the truth, for which is greater, the gift or the altar which sanctified the gift? How can you justify such hypocrisy and dishonesty in the sight of the God of heaven?* (Matthew 23:16-19)

*Woe upon you, scribes and Pharisees, and all other hypocrites! For you are scrupulous to cleanse the outside of the cup and the platter, but within there remains the filth of extortion, excesses, and deception. You are spiritually blind. Do you not recognize how much better it would be first to cleanse the inside of the cup, and then that which spills over would itself cleanse the outside? You wicked reprobates! You make the outward performances of your religion to conform with the letter of your interpretation of Moses' law while your souls are steeped in iniquity and filled with murder.* (Matthew 23:15-26, Luke 11:39-40)

One can imagine the uneasiness, the tension and the agitation building up in the majority of this congregation. No one had ever talked to them like that. They were all above reproach, they thought. What manner of man would accuse them of such hypocrisy; was he better than they?

To the hardened Pharisees, and there were many, Jesus was becoming an intolerable threat to their very existence. Just the day before, he put an end to a steady source of temple revenue by opening the cages of the sacrificial animals to be sold for the altar, and disbursed them out of the courtyard. He turned over the tables of the money changers and ran them out of the temple courtyard. A spiritual threat they might tolerate, but a threat to their temple revenues was more than they were willing to overlook. It would affect their lifestyles and their hold over the people. Although in past sermons, Jesus had clearly revealed to these men the Father's way, they were too intellectually proud and tradition bound to effectively change their ways. Now Jesus was revealing to them their sinful lifestyles and iniquitous actions and the hypocrisy of their whole rabinical system in relation to the kingdom of God. And these men resented it.

But Jesus was not through with them, as he still had more to say concerning their barren souls. Said Jesus, *Woe upon all of you who reject truth and spurn mercy! Many of you are like whited sepulchers, which outwardly appear beautiful but within are full of dead men's bones and all sorts of uncleanness. Even so do you who knowlingly reject the counsel of God appearing outwardly to men as holy and righteous, but inwardly your hearts are filled with hypocrisy and iniquity.* (Matthew 23:27-28)

*Woe upon you, false guides of a nation! Over yonder have you built a monument to the martyred prophets of old, while you plot to destroy him of whom they spoke. You garnish the tombs of the righteous and flatter yourselves that, had you lived in the days of your fathers, you would not have killed the prophets; and then in the face of such self-righteous thinking you make ready to slay him of whom the prophets spoke, the Son of Man. Inasmuch as you know these things, you are witness to yourselves that you are the wicked sons of them who slew the prophets. Go on, then and fill up the cup of your condemnation to the full!* (Matthew 23:29-32)

*Woe upon you, children of evil! John did truly call you the offspring of vipers, and I ask how can you escape the judgment that John pronounced upon you?* (Matthew 23:33)

*But even now I offer you in my Father's name mercy and forgiveness; even now I proffer the loving hand of eternal fellowship. My Father has sent you the wise men and the prophets; some you have persecuted and others you have killed. And now you make ready to shed more innocent blood. Do you not comprehend that a terrible day of reckoning will come when the judge of all earth shall require of this people an accounting for the way they have rejected, persecuted, and destroyed these messengers of heaven? Do you not understand that you must account for all this righteous blood from Abel to Zachariah whom you murdered between the sanctuary and the Altar? And if you go on in your evil ways, this accounting may be required of the new generations.* (Matthew 23:34-36, Luke 11:49-51)

*O Jerusalem, Jerusalem, and the children of Abraham, you who have stoned the prophets and killed the teachers that were sent to you, even now would I gather your children together as a hen gathers her chickens under her wings, but you are unwilling.* (Matthew 23:37, Luke 13:34)

*And now I take leave of you. You have heard my message and have made your decision. And to you who have chosen to reject the gift of God, I say that you will no more see me teaching in the temple. My work for you is done. Behold, I now go forth with my children, and your house is left to you desolate! And I say to you, from now on you shall not see me until the time comes when you say, 'Blessed is he who comes in the name of the Lord.'* (Matthew 23:38-39, Luke 13:35)

For Jesus and his followers it had been a long day, one filled with admonitions to the self-righteous and spiritually blind, but offering ample opportunity for those who would be willing to take the step of faith into the security and salvation of the kingdom of heaven.

Jesus had done all he could to reveal God's way to these hardened Jewish leaders, but they steadfastly refused to believe his revelation of the truth of God. He could do no more, so he beckoned his followers to depart from the temple.

The day, however, was far from over for his avowed enemies. That Tuesday evening of April 4, AD 30, the Sanhedrin would meet for the express purpose of dealing with Jesus.

Many times before, this supreme court of the Jewish nation had informally decreed the death of Jesus, but never before had they resolved to place him under arrest and to bring about his death at any and all cost. But on this Tuesday evening, they voted to impose the death sentence upon both Jesus and Lazarus. This was to be their answer to Jesus' last appeal to the rulers of the Jews in the temple only a few hours earlier. They bitterly resented Jesus for his vigorous indictment against them, and passing the death sentence (even before his trial) upon the Son of God was the Sanhedrin's reply to the last offer of mercy ever extended to the Jewish nation as such.

Israel had repudiated the Son of God who made a covenant with Abraham, and the plan to make the children of Abraham the light-bearers of truth to the world had been shattered. The divine covenant had been abrogated, and the Hebrew nation would soon collapse.

The officers were given orders to arrest Jesus early the next morning, and by Friday he would have been arrested without indictment; accused without evidence, adjudged without witnesses; punished without a verdict; and condemned by an unjust judge who confessed that he could find no fault in him.

This was the human fate of Jesus, a fate he chose to accept and to bear in order that all those willing to serve God may be saved.

The fate awaiting these Jewish leaders would affect their people for nearly 2,000 years. Within forty years, Jerusalem would be sacked by the Armies of Titus. Quarters would not be given and over 600,000 Jews would be slaughtered or sold as slaves. The temple would be set afire and the high priesthood and the Sanhedrin court would forever be abolished.

The Sadducees would vanish and Judaism would be reduced to a religion without a shrine, a dominate priesthood and a sacrificial service. Only the Pharisees and the rabbis would remain to lead a homeless people who had nothing left but its synagogues and its hopes.

It was a fate the Jewish people were not able to circumvent. At Jerusalem, the religious leaders had formulated the various doctrines of their traditional teachers and prophets into an established system of intellectual beliefs — a religion of authority that appealed largely to the mind. In contrast, Jesus would reveal to man a religion of the spirit as demonstrated in human experience. He would reveal to this planet a partial insight into eternal realities, a glimpse of the goodness and beauty of the infinite character of the Father in heaven. This new religion made its chief appeal to the divine spirit of the Father which resides in the mind of man, a religion which shall derive its authority from the fruits of its acceptance that will so certainly appear in the personal experience of all who choose to be spirit led.

This new religion was not intended to travel the path of certainty and intellectual settledness of the religion of traditional authority; instead, its followers had to be prepared to travel the path of uncertainty, revealing as it would, the new truths of the religion of the spirit, the kingdom of heaven in the hearts of men.

Jesus had called upon the men of his day to be born again, to be born of the spirit. He had called his people out of the darkness of authority and the lethargy of tradition into the transcendent light of a true religion of spirit, which shall be built up in the souls of men as an eternal endowment; one based upon a living faith which is able to grasp the reality of God and all that relates to the divine spirit of the Father.

The religion of his people was one of the mind, tying them hopelessly to the past. In contrast, Jesus had given them a religion of the spirit, consisting in progressive revelation designed to lead them on toward higher and holier achievements in spiritual ideals and eternal realities.

Time and again he had told them that the religion of authority can only divide men and set them in conscientious array against each other, but the religion of the spirit will progressively draw men together and cause them to become understandingly sympathetic with one another.

From the perspective of too many of the Jerusalem religious leaders, that of looking out from within, they could not see that religions of authority crystallize into lifeless creeds, but that religion of spirit grows into the increasing joy and liberty of ennobling deeds of loving service and merciful ministration.

Had these men listened to the Master, they would have come to realize that all things are sacred in the lives of those who are spirit led; that is, lives subordinated to truth, ennobled by love and dominated by mercy.

These leaders of the Jewish people and members of the

Sanhedrin refused to be spirit led and chose to discount divine truth because the channel of its bestowal was apparently human.

In less than a week they would know otherwise, but it was too late to change the fate of these people.

While the Sanhedrin court was convening to plot Jesus' apprehension, Jesus was holding his own meeting with his apostles.

After leaving the temple that late afternoon, Jesus and the twelve made their way back to the Gethsemane camp. As they passed by a project of new construction, Matthew called Jesus' attention to these beautiful buildings, asking if they were to be destroyed? And Jesus responded, *You see these stones and this massive temple; verily, verily I say to you: In the days soon to come there shall not be left one stone upon another. They shall all be thrown down.* (Matthew 24:1-2, Mark 13:1-2, Luke 21:56)

These remarks had a profound impression on the apostles, as these new buildings were of exquisite beauty and they could not conceive of any event short of the destruction of the whole world that would destroy the temple.

As they passed through the city, along the Kidron valley road towards Gethsemane, they took a shortcut by climbing the western slope of Olivet for a short distance, then followed a trail over to their private camp a short distance above the public camping grounds near Gethsemane. It was a magnificent sight standing on the western slope of Mount Olivet, just before the road turned towards Bethany, to look back upon the city with its temple illuminated in the mellow light of a full moon.

As they sat and watched the city lights in the distance, Nathaniel asked, *Tell us, Master, how shall we know when these events are about to come to pass?* (Matthew 24:13, Mark 13:34, Luke 21:7)

Answering Nathaniel's question, Jesus said, *Yes, I will tell you about the times when the people shall have filled up the cup of their iniquity; when justice shall swiftly descend upon this city of our fathers. I am about to leave you; I go to the Father. After I leave you, take heed that no man deceive you, for many will come as deliverers and will lead many astray. When you hear of wars and rumors of wars, be not troubled, for though all these things will happen, the end of Jerusalem is not yet at hand. You should not worry about famines or earthquakes; neither should you be concerned when you are delivered up to the civil authorities and are persecuted for the sake of the gospel. You will be thrown out of the synagogue and put in prison for my sake and some of you will be killed. When you are brought up before governors and rulers, it shall be for a testimony of your faith and show your steadfastness in its gospel of the kingdom. And, when you stand before judges, be not anxious beforehand as to what you should say. For I will give you utterance and wisdom as to what to say, and none of your opponents will be able to refute you.*

*In these days of travail, even your own kinsfolk, under the leadership of those who have rejected the Son of Man, will deliver you up to prison and death. For a time you may be hated by all men for my sake, but even in these persecutions I will not forsake you, my spirit will not desert you. Be patient and doubt not that this gospel of the kingdom will triumph over all enemies and eventually, be proclaimed to all nations.* (Matthew 24:4-14, Mark 13:2-13, Luke 21:8-17)

It was becoming apparent to all the apostles that some dreadful catastrophe would befall Jerusalem after Jesus' departure and that Jesus did not want them to be a part of such violent destruction. And so Andrew inquired of Jesus, asking that if the Holy City and the temple were to be destroyed, when should he and his fellows forsake Jerusalem? And Jesus replied, *You may remain in the city after I have gone, even through these times of travail and bitter persecution, but when you finally see Jerusalem being encompassed by the Roman armies after the revolt of the false prophets, then will you know that her desolation is at hand; then must you flee to the mountains. Let none who are in the city and around about tarry to save aught, neither let those who are outside dare to enter therein. There will be great tribulation, for those will be the days of Gentile vengeance. After you have deserted the city, these disobedient people will fall by the edge of the sword and will be led captive into all nations; and so shall Jerusalem be trodden down by the Gentiles.* (Matthew 24:15-21, Mark 13:14-16, Luke 21:20-24)

And then Jesus told his apostles that before the destruction of Jerusalem would take place there would be many pretenders to the throne. *In the meantime, I warn you, be not deceived. If any man comes to you saying, 'Behold, here is the Deliverer,' or 'Behold, there is he,' believe it not, for many false teachers will arise and many will be led astray but you should not be deceived, for I have told you all this beforehand.* (Matthew 24:23-25, Mark 13:21-23)

It was because of this very warning that the apostles and the entire group of believers were able to escape to the hills of Pella in the north to continue their ministry in the gospel of the kingdom.

And then Jesus told the 12 that very soon he would leave and take up the work the Father had entrusted to him, but to be of good courage, for he would sometime return. *You behold me now in weakness and flesh,* he told them, *but when I return, it shall be with power and in the spirit. The eye of flesh beholds the Son of Man in the flesh, but only the eye of the spirit will behold the Son of Man glorified by the Father and appearing on earth in his name.* (Matthew 16:27, Mark 8:38, Luke 9:26)

*But the times of the reappearing of the Son of Man is known only by the councils of Paradise; not even the angels of heaven know when this will occur.* (Matthew 24:36-42, Mark 13:32-33)

*And now concerning the travail of Jerusalem, about which I have spoken to you, even this generation will not pass away until my words are fulfilled.* (Matthew 24:34, Mark 13:30, Luke 21:32)

Then, addressing himself again to his return in the future, he told the twelve that they should be wise regarding the ripening of an age and be alert to the sign of the times. Said Jesus, *You know when the fig tree shows its tender branches and puts forth its leaves that summer is near. Likewise, when the world has passed through the long winter of material-mindedness and you discern the coming of the spiritual springtime of a new dispensation, should you know that the summertime of a new visitation draws near.* (Matthew 24:32-33, Mark 13:28-29, Luke 21:29-31)

*As individuals and as a generation of believers, hear me while I speak a parable: There was a certain great man who, before starting out on a long journey to another country, called all his trusted servants before him and delivered into their hands all his goods. To one he gave five talents, to another two, and to another one. And so down through the entire group of honored stewards to each he entrusted his goods according to their several abilities; and then he set out on his journey. When their lord had departed his servants set themselves at work to gain profits from the wealth entrusted to them. Immediately he who had received five talents began to trade with them and very soon he made a profit of another five talents. In like manner, he who had received two talents soon had gained two more. And so all of these servants made gains for their master except he who received but one talent. He went away by himself and dug a hole in the earth where he hid his lord's money. Presently, the lord of the servants unexpectedly returned and called upon his stewards for reckoning. And when they had all been called before their master, he who had received the five talents came forward with the money which had been entrusted to him and brought five additional talents, saying, 'Lord, you gave me five talents to invest, and I am glad to present five other talents as my gain.' And then his lord said to him, 'Well done, good and faithful servant, you have been faithful over a few things; I will now set you as a steward over many; enter forthwith into the joy of your lord.' And then he who had received the two talents came forward, saying: 'Lord, you delivered into my hands two talents; behold I have gained these other two talents.' And his lord then said to him: 'Well done, good and faithful steward; you also have been faithful over a few things, and I will set you over many; enter you into the joy of your lord.' And then there came to the accounting he who had received one talent. This servant came forward, saying: 'Lord, I knew you and realized that you were a shrewd man in that you expected gains where you had not personally labored; therefore, was I afraid to risk aught of that which was entrusted to me. I safely hid your talent in the earth; here it is; you now have what belongs to you. But his lord answered, 'You are an indolent and slothful steward. By your own words you confess that you knew I would require of you an accounting with reasonable profit, such as your diligent fellow servants have this day rendered. Knowing this, you ought, therefore, to have at least put my money into the hands of the bankers that on my return I might have received my own with interest.' And then to the chief steward this lord said: 'Take away this one talent from this unprofitable servant and give it to him who has the ten talents.' For everyone who has, more shall be given, and he shall have abundance; but from him who has not, even that which he has shall be taken away.* (Matthew 25:14-29)

This parable made it abundantly clear to the apostles that they were not to stand still in the affairs of the eternal kingdom; that the Father requires of his children to grow in grace and in a knowledge of the truth. And these truths must yield the increase of the fruits of the spirit and manifest a growing devotion to the unselfish service of their fellow servants. (2 Peter 3:18) *And remember,* Jesus said, *inasmuch as you minister to one of the least of my brethren, you have done this service to me.* (Matthew 25:40)

Only those faithful servants who thus grow in the knowledge of the truth, and who thereby develop a capacity for divine appreciation of spiritual realities, can ever hope to 'enter fully into the joy of their Lord.' (Matthew 25:21, 23)

In Jerusalem, the Pharisees, the proud stewards of the truth, had reduced it, segregated it, and codified it into law, whereby it had become crystallized in their minds and governed their every move. Now these same men whose minds had become saturated with prejudice and blinded by the pride of revenge were busily plotting and scheming as how best to silence this voice of truth that threatened their beliefs, their lifestyle, and their hold upon the people.

It was in the early hours of the morning that the Sadducees, who now controlled the Sanhedrin, formally decreed the death of Jesus, and having issued orders for his arrest, adjourned on this Tuesday near midnight.

As soon as they heard of his arrest, more than 30 prominent Jews who were secret believers in the kingdom met at the home of Nicodemus and decided to make open acknowledgment of their allegiance to the Master. And the next day, they did just that.

Meanwhile, Jesus was concluding his discussion with his apostles, telling them that truth is living; that the spirit of truth is ever leading the children of light into the new realms of spiritual reality and divine service; that they were not given truth to crystallize into settled, safe and honored forms.

As stewards of truth, they were not to be like the indolent, barren steward and preserve it, but to spread it and multiply its fruits. For if the endowments are used only in selfish pursuits, and no thought is bestowed upon the higher duty of obtaining increased yield of the fruits of the spirit, as they are used in the service of man and the worship of God, such selfish stewards must accept the consequences of their deliberate choosing.

As they were about to retire for the night, Jesus said to the twelve, *Freely have you received; therefore, freely should you give*

*of the truth of heaven, and in the giving will this truth multiply
and show forth the increasing light of saving grace as you minister it.* (Matthew 10:8)

And so the Master who came to us to reveal the Fatherhood
of God — that God is the loving Father of all men, even of every
single individual — and the brotherhood of man — the good will
of love and mutual trust — would be convicted this evening by
the highest Jewish court on charges that he was a dangerous
traducer of the people; that he was a fanatical revolutionist in
threatening to destroy the temple and that he taught magic
inasmuch as he promised to build a new one without hands.

After this, the longest day, Jesus would discourse one more
time with his apostles, and this "traducer of the people," this
"fanatical revolutionist" whose kingdom was founded on love,
proclaimed in mercy, and established by unselfish service, would
leave his apostles with one new commandment: *That you love
one another even as I have loved you. And by this will all men
know that you are my disciples if you thus love one another.*
(John 13:34-35)

Consistent with his teachings (John 15:13), Jesus would
soon demonstrate his greatest act of love, as exemplified by the
manner in which he would terminate his life in the flesh. He
would willingly give up his life on the cross so that whosoever
believeth in him should not perish, but have everlasting life.

# Epilogue

Although Jesus' teachings were received quite favorably by the common people of his day, the unwillingness to be spirit led by a few hardened and antagonistic religious leaders brought an abrupt end to his teaching.

Crucifixion, however, was not inevitable, as the Master could have taken up his life in the flesh in any manner he chose fit. And fittingly, he chose to submit to the natural course of events which led to his death on the cross.

Jesus desired to live a full mortal life, and when he had completed his mission as the "Son of Man," the Son of God submitted himself to the most cruel and lingering punishment a man of his day could face — crucifixion.

He had done all he could for his people. He told them that salvation was a matter of faith, and to complete the mortal drama after almost 36 years on the planet, the Son of God would end his life in the flesh, only to take it up again within 3 days to fulfill his promise to his followers and to all mankind, that salvation is real and for all who choose to do God's will.

His gospel was aimed at overcoming evil with good; his teachings centered on the brotherhood of man, the good will of love and mutual trust.

These teachings were universal, for all mankind to come to know. They were not just for the people of his day, and some, a hardened and narrow-minded few, would vehemently reject them. These were the Jewish leaders who feared his presence as a threat to their authority in subjecting their people to the written code.

It was the belief of the majority of these 71 men, the Sanhedrin court or Great Council of Elders of Israel, made up of scribes, rabbis, and priests, that rules and rituals bring man closer to God; that worship, sacrifice and strict adherence to the written laws were essential to God's favor, and to the avoidance of his wrath. God set the rules and would judge all men by them. These Jewish leaders were the keepers of the rules as given them by Moses and the prophets, and it was their duty to see that all their people abided by them. To transgress them meant accountability to the local elders and, if necessary, to the highest body of Jewish authority — the Jerusalem Sanhedrin.

Teaching of the laws and the worship of God was reserved for the synagogues and the temple. Teaching outside those places of worship was foreign to these leaders and might not only reduce the size of their congregations, but also threaten their revenues and their authority over the Jewish people. This erosion of control was their chief concern.

If the people were to believe in Jesus' teachings that *The kingdom of God is within you.* (Luke 17:21) and that God can be served outside the synagogue as well as within, maybe the prestige of these leaders would drop as the ultimate expositors and arbiters of the Jewish law.

The threat to these leaders was that Jesus was bringing God to man. Heretofore, man came to God in the temples of worship and found him in the scrolls of the Torah.

This "decentralizing of God's presence" would eventually threaten their very existence, much as it would do to the institutional church some 1,500 years later.

Jesus came at a time of relative peace on the planet, when new concepts of religious truths could gain a foothold in the minds of men. He came to a people who had come to know and to serve one God; he came to reveal, not just to these people but to all people, an expanded revelation of God's nature and his love for all his children.

It is when man or a body of men set themselves above their fellows through ecclesiastical councils and begin to set about telling others how to find God, that dissension comes about.

The Father has endowed every human mind with the faculty to discover, recognize, interpret and choose his or her own destiny through the recognition of moral values and the discernment of spiritual meanings. And this insight comes from within, not from a body of written postulates, nor from theological bodies who have become self-chosen interpreters of the rules, for the good of man.

Jesus brought to this planet the highest concept man had ever known of God the Father — a God of unbounding love and mercy. And that all man had to do on his part was to live God's will *with all his heart, and soul and mind and strength.* (Matthew 22:37)

This enlarged revelation of the Father's eternal goodness, and unbounding love for his creatures, did not require ritual

**214**

cleansing of the body, only purification of the soul by striving to do God's will; it did not require ceremonial sacrifice at the temple for sins committed, but a recognition in the citadel of the mind that God forgives us of our sins when we forgive those who have sinned against us. It did not require the formulation of written laws by which to live in order to prevent God's wrath, only a living faith and complete trust in God to ensure our salvation. Man was not to judge the religiosity of his fellow man, for he can only judge his fellow man by his deeds; only God can judge by intent. And lastly, man's spiritual accountability was not to man, or to anybody of authority except God himself. God is no respecter of persons; to him the humblest and the poorest of men has as much right to enter the kingdom as the Pharisees and the rich. For the kingdom is a place for men's hearts. All one needed to enter was faith; to progress in it, one needed to serve others.

Jesus was a master at serving others. He literally went about doing good, bringing joy and comfort to all he met. He was always willing to stop a sermon just to minister to a single person, even a little child. His ministry was always positive and appealed to the better things in human nature. The Master taught that love consumes fear, that spiritual insight — religious faith — brightens the soul, while removing the darkened apprehensions of uncertainty.

To the Jewish leaders in Jesus' day, the Laws of Moses governed their every action. These stern, judgmental, Scripture-quoting Pharisees inflicted their flocks with negative postulates. They were more concerned with what man shouldn't do than with what he could do. But moral worth cannot be derived from mere repression, and "thou shall nots" ruled the day.

Although possessing those attributes of love and mercy, God was more to be feared than to be loved. His laws were not to be transgressed, for he was a God of wrath and vengeance.

These Jewish leaders feared to travel off the path of tradition; they steadfastly refused to examine the path of faith. They knew the word, but never permitted the word to get in them, trying to obey God's laws without knowing God's love. Consumed with gathering the "dry sands of knowledge," they neglected to "water the garden of their hearts."

The scribes, Pharisees and the priesthood held the Jews in a terrible bondage of ritualism and legalism far worse than

Roman political rule, with the threat that if the laws of the prophets were not adhered to in the strictest of detail, surely the Jewish people would suffer greater consequences than the days of Babylonian captivity — total destruction.

Had the Jewish leaders followed the admonition of the Master to "Render under Caesar that which is Caesar's," surely their fate would have been different. Failing to address their religious yoke, certain factions instead concentrated on removing Rome's political yoke, an effort that would eventually result in the total destruction of Jerusalem and the demise of the Jewish nation for almost 2,000 years. The same authoritative ecclesiastical rule that faced the Jewish people in Jesus' day would manifest itself in Christendom some 1,500 years after the Diaspora, whereupon a number of reformists would seek to remove Rome's theocratic yoke upon all Christians. They succeeded.

In presenting the gospel of the kingdom — the Fatherhood of God and the Brotherhood of Man — Jesus had come to live among his people and to teach by example, revealing as he did God's love and compassion for all mankind. To follow Jesus means to personally share his religious faith and to enter into the spirit of the Master's life of unselfish service for man. But this new religion required of man a strong will, one of unfailing confidence to believe what Jesus believed and as he believed. The requisite of this new gospel was not intellectual assuredness, as in the knowledge of the laws of the elders, but faith, faith as that of a little child. *Except you become as a little child, you shall not enter the kingdom.* (Matthew 18:3, Mark 10:15, Luke 18:17)

This simply meant a subordination of man's will, to God's will. By subordinating man's will to the divine will, man was putting trust in God, and by trusting God, man had to no longer worry about God's anger nor his wrath to come, for he had put his faith in God's hands. As a child's faith begins to grow, fear and apprehension diminish proportionately, yielding to the joy of personal security in the heavenly Father's overcare.

But this expanded revelation of the Father's love was too foreign for the Jewish leaders to accept. Their religion of the mind would not submit to a religion of the heart. It was deeds that counted, as they could be observed and weighed by both man and God. But faith, how could anyone measure a man's faith?

Although they would not admit it, these Jewish religious leaders had evolved a religion of pretensions based upon proper conduct and ceremonial observances. Public recognition of alms giving was important to them and they carried trumpets at their sides for just such occasions. Being seen at stately banquets and holding seats of high honor near the host elevated their egos and enhanced their prestige among the people. Being able to purchase the more expensive animals to be sacrificed at the feasts served to set them apart from the multitudes of mediocrity.

The majority of these Sanhedrin leaders knew their place among men, and that was apart and higher than most. All too many of them were proud and self-righteous, to the point of religious arrogance. They had elevated themselves above the common man and looked disdainfully upon other peoples, especially the Samaritans. But even the "cynics" of their day knew that "the man who knows God looks upon all men as equal; that they are his brethren."

These Sanhedrin leaders could not see that "pride obscures God" and that "the spirit of the true God is in man's heart." They were too enmeshed in ceremonialism — fasting frequently, working sedulously, and observing the oral traditions.

Of the two religious parties, only the Pharisees, who lived the more simple life, would survive the Diaspora. Upon the destruction of the temple (AD 70), the priesthood and the Sadducees faded into oblivion.

Although a number of barren souls did their best to deny and reject Jesus' teachings, there were others who suffered persecution and died for their new faith.

To those who chose to hear it, his message was clear and simple, proclaiming spiritual liberty, teaching eternal truth and fostering living faith. His kingdom was founded on love, proclaimed in mercy and established by unselfish service. And the Master lived just such a life of loving service in the brotherhood of man, "dispensing health and happiness, naturally and gracefully as he journeyed through life."

Although his life and teachings were for all men and all generations, not all men followed him. And that, said Jesus, was *because they do not know the one who sent me.* (John 15:21) *He who hates me hates my Father also.* (John 15:23) Rejecting Jesus was rejecting God. And he told his apostles, as he would be persecuted so would they. (John 15:20)

It was to these followers he would show himself after the Resurrection. From the early hours of that glorious Sunday morning, April 9, AD 30, when Jesus appeared to Mary Magdalene, and for some forty days thereafter, he would reveal himself only to those believers who had accepted his gospel message before his crucifixion. For he said in the flesh, *While you have the light, believe in the light.* (John 12:36) When those who sprewned the Kingdom when he came in the likeness of humanity, sought to find entrance when he was revealed in the likeness of divinity, it would be too late. To all such selfish ones when they came knocking, Jesus would say, *I know not where you are from.* (Luke 12:25)

Now in glorified form, the Master would tell his apostles, *He who has believed and has been baptized shall be saved . . .* (Mark 16:16) *Because you have seen me have you believed. Blessed are they who did not see and yet believed.* (John 20:29)

These apostles were chosen by their Lord, and they gave all that could humanly be expected of them. Having spent a season with him, they knew better than any man that Jesus was *the way, the truth and the life.* (John 14:6) And they went about spreading the gospel with the confidence and assurance that Jesus was with them, for the Master said he would send them a part of himself — The Spirit of Truth — who would aid and comfort them in their ministry. (John 14:167-18)

And then before he departed from these hearty Galileans, the Master said, *As the Father has loved me so have I loved you. Live in my love even as I live in the Father's love. If you do as I have taught you, you shall abide in my love even as I have kept the Father's word and evermore abide in his love.* (John 15:9-10)

And they did just that. When John, the last of the apostles, was no longer able to stand in the pulpit and preach, he had to be carried to church in a chair, and when at the close of the services he was asked to say a few words to the believers he would only say, *My little children, love one another.*

# Gospel Writers

**John Mark** had the opportunity of few young men, having spent a season traveling with Jesus and the apostles while still a young lad of no more than 14 or 15 years of age. With his parents' consent, he traveled with the apostles experiencing first-hand many of their encounters with the populous. At the instigation of Peter, and upon the request of the church at Rome, Mark undertook the writing of the briefest and most simple account of Jesus' life. This was the first gospel completed in the year AD 68, which Mark wrote entirely from his own memory and from Peter's memory. In reality, it is the Gospel of Simon Peter which depicts Jesus as a minister among men.

**Matthew Levi's** gospel was written for the edification of Jewish Christians. It portrays Jesus as a son of David, and shows great respect for the law and the prophets. Although actually written by his disciple, Isador, who wrote in Greek, Matthew provided the outline from his notes written in Aramaic. It was not until the armies of Titus had destroyed Jerusalem that Matthew commissioned Isador to write his gospel. It was in the hills of Pella, in the year AD 71, that Matthew's narrative was written.

**John Zebedee,** in the year AD 101 (some 70 years after Jesus' death), directed Nathan, a Greek Jew from Caesarea, to write his gospel. John wrote a cover letter known as the Epistle of "First John" for Nathan, who executed the work under John's direction. Towards the end of his years, John was quite feeble and was cared for by a loving daughter. Called "the Apostle who would never die," John eventually died from old age in the year AD 103 at 101 years of age. This gospel relates much of the work Jesus did in Judea and around Jerusalem which is not contained in other records. Years earlier, when in temporary exile on the Aegean isle of Patmos, John wrote the Book of Revelation.

**Luke,** a physician of Antioch in Pesidia, was a Gentile convert of Paul and wrote his gospel depicting Jesus as a friend of publicans and sinners. He began to follow Paul in the late 40's and gathered much information about Jesus from scores of eyewitnesses over the next 30 years. It was not until after Paul's death that Luke actually sat down in the year AD 82, in Anchaia, near Corinth in Greece, to write his gospel. He had copies of both Mark's gospel and Matthew's gospel, as well as notes of Andrew and others, in which to substantiate his narrative. He died in the year AD 90, just before he finished the second of three planned works — the "Acts of the Apostles."

# Political Personalities

**Annas** — the chief ecclesiastical authority and the most powerful single individual in all Jewry, maintained his palace on Mount Olivet, not far from the Garden of Gethsemane. Although no longer the chief high priest, it was customary for the Roman authorities to deal with Annas first on any and all delicate matters. He was a suave, politic planner and desired to direct the matter of disposing of Jesus. It was to Annas Jesus was first sent for questioning, and it was Annas who directed the Master's trial and execution.

**Caiaphas** — the brash, impetuous and arrogant son-in-law of Annas. An acting high priest who had gathered some 30 members of the Sanhedrin court in his palace to sit in judgment of Jesus, after he had been detained and interrogated by Annas for some 3 hours. Shortly before the trial was to begin, his father-in-law, Annas, arrived and took his seat beside Caiaphas to direct the proceedings.

**Herod the Great** — called King of the Jews, was no Jew at all, but an Idumean hailing from the land south of Judea. Nevertheless, having ingratiated himself years earlier with the Roman authorities, he was the political overseer to the Jews, accountable to the Legate of Syria and to the emperor himself.

During his life he had a total of 10 wives and 14 children. His second wife, Marianne, was the granddaughter of Hyrcannes II and sister of Aristobulus, both of whom Herod had slain. He also sentenced two sons by Marianne to death, as well as Antipater, the son of his first wife. It was Herod who decreed the death of all boy babies under two years of age in Bethlehem, the order of which was executed in October of 6 BC. Before his death in 4 BC, Herod had divided his kingdom among his remaining three sons. To Philip went the eastern region known as Batanea. To Herod Antipas went Perea and, in the north, Galilee; and to Archelaus fell Samaria, Idumea and Judea. He was 69 when he died, and hated by all his people. It was said of him by his enemies that "he stole to the throne like a fox, ruled like a tiger and died like a dog."

**Archelaus** — from the very beginning of his rule (5 BC), he was at odds with the rulers of Jerusalem. When the councils of Hillel declared a revolt against his rule, he had 3,000 of these

Jewish nationals slain, most of whom had come to Jerusalem for the Passover. Less than two months later, at the feast of Pentecost, many more suffered great slaughter. As the situation worsened, many Jews killed themselves in despair, prompting a delegation of leading Jews to journey to Rome to have Archelaus removed as tetrarch of Judea. He was removed by Augustus in AD 6, and Judea was made a Roman province of the second class, under the procurator responsible to the governor of Syria.

**Herod Antipas** — when in Jerusalem, would stay in the old Maccobean palace of his father, Herod the Great. As tetrarch of Galilee, this wicked Idumean had decreed that, if Jesus were to enter his domain, he was to be apprehended. Herod feared Jesus ever since he beheaded John the Baptist. Although he had no jurisdiction over Jesus in Judea, he was quite relieved when the Master was taken into custody by the palace guards of Pilate, knowing that it was Pilate's responsibility to put him to death.

**Pontius Pilate** — the procurator of Judea, began his rule in the year AD 26, when Jesus was 31½-years-old. (The same year Jesus was baptized.) He was a weak man with a deep-seated hatred for his Jewish subjects. Of all Roman provinces, none was more difficult to rule than Judea. Pilate never took seriously the deep-seated prejudice of the Jews against all images as symbols of idol worship. He would therefore allow his soldiers to enter Jerusalem without removing the images of Caesar from their banners, an act the Jews deeply resented. When they implored him to have these images removed, he answered by threatening them with death.

When the Jewish leaders brought Jews to Pilate, he tried to circumvent his responsibility by sending the Master to Herod, who clearly had no jurisdiction in Judea. When forced to confront the situation, he cowardly backed down, allowing Jesus to be taken by his enemies to safeguard his personal position. He was finally deposed as a result of the needless slaughter of Samaritans. He was ordered to Rome by the Legate of Syria, but Tiberius died while he was enroute. He was not reappointed as procurator of Judea and, finding no favor with the new emperor, he retired to the province of Lausanne, where he subsequently committed suicide. His wife, Claudia Procula eventually became a believer in the gospel of the kingdom.

# Suggested Reading

Alon, Azarin. *Natural History of the Land of the Bible.* Garden City, New York, Doubleday & Co., 1978.

Asch, Sholem. *The Nazarene.* New York, Putnam & Sons, 1939.

Bates, E. S., Ed. *Bible Designed to Be Read As Living Literature.* New York, Simon & Schuster, 1952.

Bruce, A. B. *The Training of the Twelve.* 3rd Ed., New York, Richard R. Smith, Inc., 1930.

Bruce, F.F. *The New Testament Documents: Are They Reliable?* 5th Ed., Grand Rapids, Michigan, William Eardman Publishing Co., 1960.

Bruin, Paul. *Jesus Lived Here.* Translated by William Neil, New York, William Marlow & Co., 1958.

Corswant, W. *A Dictionary of Life in Bible Times.* New York, Oxford University Press, 1960.

Daniel-Rops, Henri. *Daily Life in the Times of Jesus.* Ann Arbor, Michigan, Servant Books, 1962.

Dean, Anthony. *The World Christ Knew.* E. Lansing, Michigan, State Press, 1953.

Edersheim, Alfred. *The Life of Jesus, the Messiah.* London, Longmans, Greem & Co., 1901.

Filson, Floyd V. *The New Testament Against Its Environment.* London; SCM Press Ltd., 1950.

Josephus. *Complete Works.* Translated by William Whiston, Grand Rapids, Michigan, Kregel Publishing, 1960.

Jeremais, Joachim. *Rediscovering the Parables.* New York, Charles Scribner's Sons, 1966.

Lamsa, George. *The Gospel Light.* Philadelphia, A. J. Holman Co., 1964.

Moore, George Foot. *Judaism.* Cambridge, Massachusetts, Harvard University Press, 1927, 2 Vols.

Morgan, G. Campbell. *The Crisis of the Christ.* New York, Fleming H. Revell Co., 1930.

Morgan, G. Campbell. *The Teaching of Christ.* New York, Fleming H. Revell, 1913.

Morton, H. V.. *In the Steps of the Master.* 23rd Ed., London, Methuen & Co., 1953.

National Geographic Society. *Everyday Life in Ancient Times.* Washington, DC, National Geographic Society, 1958.

Pax, W. E. *In the Footsteps of Jesus*. Jerusalem, Israel, Nateev Publishers, 1970.

Pfeiffer, Robert H. *History of the New Testament Times*. New York, Harper & Brothers, 1949.

Readers Digest. *Jesus and His Times*. New York, 1987.

Stevens, William Arnold. *A Harmony of the Gospels*. Boston, Silver, Burdett & Co., 1897.

Thompson, John A. *Archaeology and the New Testament*. Grand Rapids, Michigan, William Erdmans Publishing Co., 1960.

Trench, Richard C. *Notes on the Miracles of Our Lord*. 11th Ed., London, Macmillan & Co., 1878.

Wright, G. Ernest. *Biblical Archaeology*. Philadelphia, Westminster Press, 1960.

## About the Author

Walter Ziglar, author and educator, is a native of Southern California and a graduate of the University of Southern California. He is currently the trustee for the United Methodist Church of Corona del Mar, California.

In 1971, recognizing the need for a competent college preparatory school in the greater Los Angeles area, he founded the Brentwood School, the first co-educational, independent, secondary school in Los Angeles. Today it is the largest school of its kind in Southern California.

In the mid-seventies, while serving as Brentwood's president, Mr. Ziglar helped a friend establish his budding herb tea company. Eventually, he entrusted the school to his board of trustees and set out for China and the Caucusus region of USSR to research herbs that might be used for new teas.

During his travels, he became aware of one particular herb similar to American ginseng. His research of the herb led to the publication of his first book, "The Ginseng Report," a critical evaluation of commercial ginseng products sold in the United States.

In the early 1980's, Mr. Ziglar created a reading by phonics game, a remedial reading program to assist poor readers in developing better reading skills in Orange County.

Pursuing his doctorate in education at his own pace, Walter has had time to pursue his first love —research and writing — this time on a subject close to his heart — the life and teachings of Jesus.